Palm® Pre™

FOR

DUMMIES®

Palm® Pre™ FOR DUMMIES®

by Chris Ziegler

WILEY

Wiley Publishing, Inc.

Palm® Pre™ For Dummies®

Published by
Wiley Publishing, Inc.
111 River Street
Hoboken, NJ 07030-5774

www.wiley.com

Copyright © 2009 by Wiley Publishing, Inc., Indianapolis, Indiana

Published by Wiley Publishing, Inc., Indianapolis, Indiana

Published simultaneously in Canada

For general information on our other products and services, please contact our Customer Care Department within the U.S. at 877-762-2974, outside the U.S. at 317-572-3993, or fax 317-572-4002.

For technical support, please visit www.wiley.com/techsupport.

Wiley also publishes its books in a variety of electronic formats. Some content that appears in print may not be available in electronic books.

Library of Congress Control Number: 2009935830

ISBN: 978-0-470-52689-7

Manufactured in the United States of America

10 9 8 7 6 5 4 3 2 1

WILEY

About the Author

Chris Ziegler is a mobile enthusiast who can rarely be spotted using the same phone twice. Although his passions include driving, flying, motorcycling, and pretty much anything that involves gasoline, he's usually piloting nothing more than his own computer as an editor for the technology blog Engadget. A native of Michigan, he currently lives in Chicago with two Macs, two PCs, and a pile of portable devices taller than himself.

Dedication

To my awesome parents, who work tirelessly to make sure that I'm sleeping from time to time.

Author's Acknowledgments

My deep gratitude to Katie Mohr and Tiffany Ma for believing in the book and cracking the whip when needed; to Mark Enochs and Teresa Artman for making sure I made sense; and to Sandy Berger and Elaine Marmel for stepping in and stepping up. This book was a labor of love for the Palm Pre, and it couldn't have happened without them!

Publisher's Acknowledgments

We're proud of this book; please send us your comments through our online registration form located at http://dummies.custhelp.com. For other comments, please contact our Customer Care Department within the U.S. at 877-762-2974, outside the U.S. at 317-572-3993, or fax 317-572-4002.

Some of the people who helped bring this book to market include the following:

Acquisitions and Editorial

Senior Project Editor: Mark Enochs

Acquisitions Editor: Katie Mohr

Senior Copy Editor: Teresa Artman

Technical Editor: Sandy Berger

Editorial Manager: Leah Cameron

Editorial Assistant: Amanda Graham

Senior Editorial Assistant: Cherie Case

Cartoons: Rich Tennant
(www.the5thwave.com)

Composition Services

Project Coordinators: Katie Crocker, Sheree Montgomery

Layout and Graphics: Ana Carrillo, Christin Swinford

Proofreaders: John Greenough, C.M. Jones, Jessica Kramer

Indexer: Potomac Indexing, LLC

Special Help: Tiffany Ma, Elaine Marmel, and Jennifer Riggs

Publishing and Editorial for Technology Dummies

    Richard Swadley, Vice President and Executive Group Publisher

    Andy Cummings, Vice President and Publisher

    Mary Bednarek, Executive Acquisitions Director

    Mary C. Corder, Editorial Director

Publishing for Consumer Dummies

    Diane Graves Steele, Vice President and Publisher

Composition Services

    Gerry Fahey, Vice President of Production Services

    Debbie Stailey, Director of Composition Services

Contents at a Glance

Table of Contents

Introduction

*H*ello, and a hearty welcome to *Palm Pre For Dummies!* This book has been written with absolutely everyone in mind. Whether you're a new Pre owner, a longtime Pre user (dare I say Pre fanatic?), just looking for some quick pointers — or you're simply trying to decide whether the Pre is right for you — this book can take you where you need to go.

But first, perhaps a little background is in order: just what is the Pre, exactly? Palm is a longtime veteran of the electronic organizer and smartphone industries, and there's a good chance you've owned a Palm device in the past or know someone who does. Pre is the first Palm smartphone, though, to run an entirely new operating system — webOS — which was built from the ground up to power some of the most attractive and easiest-to-use smartphones in the world.

webOS is a revolutionary mobile OS for a number of reasons that you'll discover throughout this book, but allow me to touch on a few of the key points here.

- ✔ **webOs and Synergy.** First, webOS employs something that Palm calls *Synergy,* which is a technology that you'll hear me echo countless times in the chapters ahead because it's so central to everything that webOS is about. In brief, Synergy seeks to collect information from dozens of sources in your life and pool them into a single place — your phone. Why should you have to go to one application to access your Gmail and another to access your corporate e-mail? Why should you have to look through three different address books to find that long-lost friend? You shouldn't, and Synergy is there to help.

- ✔ **webOS is beautiful!** It's not often that a company has the opportunity to design something as fundamental as an OS from the ground up, and Palm certainly didn't squander that opportunity: It's a truly visually stunning experience. Everything from the fonts to the rounded corners of visual elements was exquisitely and painstakingly designed to be appealing to the eye.

- ✔ **webOS fundamentally rethinks how we use our phones.** Certain portions of the OS are unique in the mobile world, and I can guarantee you haven't seen things done quite this way before. Take Card View, for example (which I cover like a glove in Chapter 3), the interesting and unique way to effortlessly manage multiple applications at the same time.

Beyond webOS, of course, there's the Pre itself. When closed, the phone is unlike any phone you've ever seen: black, glossy, streamlined, and seemingly without buttons or controls of any sort. (Actually, it's possible you've seen *rocks* that look like that before, but never a phone!) Slide the Pre open, though, and you've suddenly got a fantastic QWERTY keyboard that helps to make the phone one of the most productive mobile e-mail machines on the market today.

But odds are good that I don't need to sell you on the virtues of the Pre. You probably already own one, in which case you're going to be amazed at some of the incredible things you can do with your portable workhorse over the course of this book. And if you *don't* own a Pre yet, well, let me just say that I wouldn't be surprised if you did by the time you got a few chapters in!

About This Book

Palm Pre For Dummies can be read from beginning to end, and if you're just getting started with the Pre, I recommend that you approach this book exactly that way. And if you haven't purchased a Pre yet, that's not a problem at all; you can hop around to whatever topics interest you. You'll find a ton of figures to help you understand how different portions of webOS work, and you won't need a Pre sitting in front of you to enjoy them!

While I'd be honored and delighted if you read *Palm Pre For Dummies* cover-to-cover — and I'm pretty sure you'd enjoy every last word of it — I understand that you might be in a hurry to get straight to the information you need.

If you're comfortable with the basic concepts of navigating around your Pre, getting between applications, and performing basic tasks, you can safely skip Chapters 1– 3. If you're a pro at making and receiving calls, you can skip Chapter 4 although you might want to skim it to pick up some tips on managing text messages.

Down the road, after you've become a Pre User Extraordinaire, I hope this book takes on an entirely different lease in life. Look to it as a reference — a guide that you can pull out the next time you need to remember how to open a link in a new card in the Browser or create a new e-mail account.

Even after your Pre takes its last call and embarks on its fateful journey to the recycling center, not all is lost. webOS is here to stay, and if you purchase another webOS phone, you'll find that much of this book is every bit as useful then as it is today. Talk about the gift that keeps on giving!

Conventions Used in This Book

Over the course of the book, you'll notice there are a few terms to keep in mind. Don't worry; I won't make you memorize words like *sesquipedalian*. Here's some basic Pre vocabulary:

- The Pre has a *Center button* placed directly below the screen. It also has *keys* on the slide-out QWERTY keyboard. There will be times when I ask you to *push* or *press* the Center button and these keys.

- Speaking of keys, you'll notice that one of them in the lower left is orange. This — surprise, surprise — is the *Orange key*. By holding it down, you'll use it to type the numbers and symbols that appear above the letters on each key.

- The Pre has *icons* and *buttons* that appear on the screen. If I ask you to *tap* them, you should touch them briefly with your finger and then release.

- I refer to various *gestures* in the book. A gesture is a motion that you make with your finger on or below the screen. Check out Chapter 3 for the lowdown on all the gestures you'll be needing in your Pre-filled travels.

- I will sometimes talk about returning to *Card View*. Card View is essentially your home base while using the Pre — it's a place where you can go to quickly launch applications and see all of the applications that are running. These applications will appear as *cards*. See Chapter 3 for a thorough rundown on using Card View.

- At times, I talk about a specific *screen*. That is, not literally the Pre's screen, but a specific display of information, such as the Preferences & Accounts screen in the Email application.

The Lay of the Land: How This Book Is Organized

Palm Pre For Dummies is divided into five separate (but equal!) parts, each roughly covering a part of the Pre's personality. Because the Pre so effortlessly crosses boundaries and mixes work with pleasure, some of these boundaries are fuzzy, but I did my best.

Part I: Introducing webOS and the Palm Pre

Because webOS is such a wide new world of functionality — which for many of you will be completely unlike anything you've ever seen or used — Part I is all about introducing some of the concepts that make webOS what it is. I talk about the physical features of the Pre, how to get between applications, how to use *cards* (Pre-speak for an open application), and how to use some of the finger gestures that will get you through every nook and cranny of the OS.

Part II: All About Communicating

It's a phone, so the Pre is really all about communicating, right? Indeed, Part II takes you through phone calls, messages of all sorts, and e-mail. You'll also discover more in Part II about one of the most incredible features of webOS — Synergy — which helps the Pre to organize text messages, multimedia messages, and instant messages (like AIM and Google Talk) into a single place.

Part III: Organizing Your Life

Now that you know how to contact your friends, you've got to know how to plan nights out on the town with them, right? In Part III, I break down some of the organizational features of the Pre like the Calendar. You'll also see how to manage every aspect of your Contacts list. And when you get all that information entered, you'll be able to search it like a pro by learning about the Pre's Universal Search capability.

Part IV: Staying Connected and Playing with the Pre

Alright, now that you have the business end of the Pre under your belt, it's time to loosen the tie and have some fun! In Part IV, you'll check out some of the fun stuff that makes the Pre such a great companion: music, the camera, real-time navigation, Web browsing, and more. And when you finally get bored of the software that comes installed on the Pre (trust us; it'll take you a while), I show you how to go and get *more* apps!

Part V: The Part of Tens

No *For Dummies* book would be complete without the Part of Tens! In *Palm Pre For Dummies*, I show you ten of our favorite applications (that you just learned how to install in Part IV, by the way) and give you a quick look at some great accessories you can use to personalize your Pre and make it truly your own.

Icons Used in This Book

Tips are the things that'll make you loudly exclaim, "Huh! I didn't know that!" while you're reading and make everyone around you look at you kinda funny. All kidding aside, though, I put together some of my favorite time-savers and labeled them as tips, so keep an eye out for this symbol.

Obviously, in a perfect world, you'd remember everything in every book you ever read! Every once in a while, though, I'll write something that I really think you should keep in mind, so I label it with this icon. Commit it to memory!

If you see this icon, it's usually because peril isn't far away. Watch out for these — they could save you some trouble.

Sometimes there's some extra information of a technical nature that you might find interesting but isn't critical to your understanding of the material. For stuff like that, look for this icon.

So, What's Next?

As the old saying goes, "The Pre's your oyster." Okay, maybe that isn't an old saying, but you get the idea — the phone is just waiting for you to explore it, and I'm here to help. Dive right into Chapter 1 if you want a fresh start, or if you want to chart your own course and dive into the book as you run into questions while you play around on the Pre, simply use the table of contents and index as your guides. I'll be right here when you me.

Part I

Introducing webOS and the Palm Pre

"This model comes with a particularly useful function — a simulated static button for breaking out of long-winded conversations."

In this part . . .

There's a lot of history built into each and every Palm Pre that rolls off the assembly line — but there's a lot of thoroughly modern, powerful, gee-whiz technology, too. In Chapter 1, I start off by making sure you and your Pre have been formally introduced. I show you how the Pre came to be (users of older Palm devices will especially appreciate this part), and I talk about the all-new operating system — *webOS* — that powers the Pre.

In Chapters 2 and 3, you'll find out how to feed and care for your Pre (geek-speak for "charge the phone"), turn it on, and get around the powerful new user interface. These chapters are especially important (and especially fun) for understanding how to navigate all the awesome applications you'll discover throughout the book, so grab a cup of hot cocoa and settle in!

Chapter 1

Your Palm Pre: The Pre-fect Phone

*1*f you're reading this book, odds are very good that you have a slick, glossy, beautifully crafted, compact smartphone in your hand or pocket, or sitting on the desk next to you (conspicuously placed so that passers-by can gawk and ask questions, of course). And I can't say that I blame you for getting a Pre. Palm's latest handset (cell, phone, whatever you want to call it) is widely regarded to be the best-looking gadget the company has ever made — and arguably, it's one of the best-looking smartphones ever made by any company, period.

Of course, looks aren't everything (supermodels, movie stars, and purveyors of $300 haircuts can disagree, but then again, they're not writing this book). Long gone are the days when a phone could simply do a decent job of making calls and sending the occasional text message. Chances are that you're spending nearly as much time fiddling with your phone as you are with your computer, if not more. You expect it perform as the consummate electronic helpmate to organize your life; entertain you; and connect you with the people, places, and things that matter to you most.

Most importantly, your phone has to be simple and intuitive to use. After all, what's the point of a phone that can send e-mail if it's too much trouble to compose a new message in the amount of time it takes you to run between your 9 o'clock and 10 o'clock meetings? For starters, an easy-to-use interface and a full QWERTY keyboard would help, wouldn't they?

Fortunately, Palm's product line was founded on a couple of very basic principles:

✔ These devices should be small enough to fit in your pocket (and durable enough so that they won't break while they're there). Check!

> ✔ These devices should make your life simpler, not more complicated. Double check!
>
> ✔ These devices should be affordable. Triple check!

And although the Pre bears little resemblance to its predecessors in Palm's rich lineage, those principles remain as true today as they ever have. And as you embark on your magical journey through this book, you'll find out exactly why that is.

How the Pre Came to Be

To really understand how the Pre came into this world, go back — way back, in fact, to the formative years of the so-called personal digital assistant (PDA). (See Figure 1-1.) In the early 1990s, companies like Apple were experimenting with portable devices — *long* before the iPhone, mind you — that could hold your contacts, appointments, and documents in one portable device that went everywhere you did. The look to the future was that such gadgets would eventually become standard equipment in every business-person's (and every consumer's) arsenal.

Figure 1-1:
An early PDA (the Apple Newton) and a sleek, sexy Pre.

These forethinking companies were right, of course. PDAs and PDA-like gadgets would eventually gain tremendous popularity among the young and old alike, but this wouldn't happen exactly the way these companies envisioned. The problem was that these first PDAs were heavy, frequently too big to slip into a jacket or pants pocket, often required many hours of training to use correctly, and were devastatingly expensive, putting them out of reach of virtually anyone who couldn't foot the bill with a corporate expense account.

That's where Palm came into play. The company's first models (PalmPilots) were released in 1996 and totally bucked the trend set by Apple and others. All Palm wanted to do was make a cheap, tiny organizer that could effectively manage the information you needed to make it through a day, run forever (not literally, but almost) on a single set of alkaline batteries, and sync your calendar effortlessly with your computer so that you could have your information at your fingertips regardless of whether you were at your desk or on the road. It was a brilliant concept, and Palm sold these first models by the boatloads.

Eventually, Palm's founders wanted to stretch their legs and try something new. They left the company they helped create to start a new one — Handspring — which made more advanced PDAs incorporating innovations like color screens, using Palm's software.

Over time, Handspring got into the business of creating smartphones, which at the time were almost unheard of. Many people hadn't even yet begun to carry a cellphone of *any* sort, let alone a smart one. It was a bold move that led to the creation of the first Treo smartphones that elegantly combined Palm's established software, a phone, and attractive design in a single gadget. Treo went on to become one of the most successful smartphone brands in history, and odds are good that you've owned one or two in the past ten years — I know I have!

Palm knew a good thing when it saw one and ended up buying Handspring, reuniting the company's founders and bringing the Treo line of phones into its own product portfolio. In an effort to strengthen the business, the company split into two separate firms: PalmSource, focusing on the Palm OS software; and palmOne, focusing on the actual PDA and smartphone hardware.

Of course, nothing ever works out quite the way you expect it to, does it? PalmSource ended up being purchased by the Japanese firm ACCESS, and palmOne (which eventually changed its name back to Palm — go figure) gravitated toward the competing Windows Mobile software from Microsoft. Palm eventually stopped making PDAs altogether to concentrate on its smartphone business, but with fierce competition from the Apple iPhone, BlackBerry, and others, it was unclear how it'd manage, especially without a modern OS of its own.

Palm knew it needed a change to stay on top of its game — a *big* change. It had to create a really awesome smartphone, and an even more awesome OS to underpin it. It took a couple of years, but the groundbreaking Pre was ultimately introduced in January of 2009 — and released in June of 2009 — along with Palm's all-new operating system, webOS. You can see the significant look and feel in Figure 1-2). Finally, after years of floundering, Palm had returned to its roots.

It's an exciting time to own a Palm again!

Pre and webOS: Like peanut butter and jelly

There's an important distinction between the Pre and the OS under its hood: webOS. Just like Palm OS in the good ol' days, webOS can run on a variety of devices — not just the Pre. At the time of this writing, the Pre is the only webOS device available, but that's not to say that you won't be able to pick from 2 or 5 or even 20 webOS-powered smartphones down the road.

So, a lot of what you can glean about the Pre from this book and from experience using the phone will be transferrable to other webOS phones that you might buy in the future. You won't have to relearn basic tasks, which is a nice little bonus. Palm has said that webOS is its platform of choice for the next decade, so your expertise will be useful for many years to come. It also means that this book shouldn't see a recycling bin for a *long* time, so keep it around as a reference, even if your Pre is long gone!

---

webOS

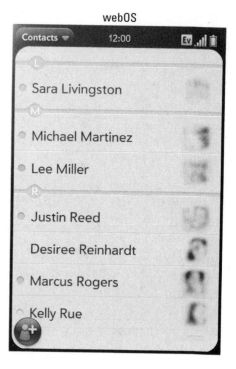

Palm OS

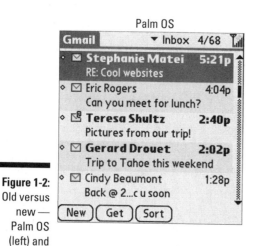

Figure 1-2:
Old versus
new —
Palm OS
(left) and
webOS
(right).

The Truth behind webOS

To be sure, the Pre is a great-looking, great-feeling, nimble phone, but the real story at Palm these days is the all-new software that powers the Pre: webOS. Here are some of the big stand-out features that make webOS special.

Linux-based

Like Windows and Mac OS X, Linux is a powerful, secure OS capable of underpinning some of the world's most high-performance servers, desktop PCs, and laptops. Linux, renowned for its versatility, has been adapted for use on everything from cable boxes to the GPS system in your car. For you, it means that webOS already comes built-in with 20 years of bug fixes, performance improvements, and enhanced features thanks to the work that's been done in the Linux programmer community.

Programmed like the Web

You probably won't notice it, but most applications that you use on your Pre are based on the same technologies that power the Web — HTML, JavaScript, CSS, and the like. That means that it's easier and faster than ever for developers to create smartphone applications, so even if the App Catalog seems a bit light at the moment, you should be seeing a plethora of exciting programs become available for your Pre in record time.

Open to you, application developers, and the world

Palm provides interested developers with all the tools they need to develop apps, but Palm goes one step further and offers to the public much of the code used to create webOS. By allowing developers to see this code, they can better understand how it works, which helps them create better apps of their own and point out potential flaws to Palm that can be fixed with an operating system software update. And speaking of operating system software updates, keep reading.

Over-the-air (OTA) updates

Some smartphones (ahem; most notably the iPhone) need to connected to a computer to be updated. In webOS, however, application updates and OS updates can be performed using your wireless signal alone. That means that you'll have the latest, greatest version of webOS available faster (and with less effort). In fact, the Pre will automatically update itself!

A revolutionary user interface

Unless the Pre is your very first smartphone (in which case, welcome to the club!), you've already seen what a typical smartphone's UI looks like. And I can guarantee you that regardless of whether you're coming from an iPhone, a Windows Mobile phone, a BlackBerry phone, or any other phone, you've never seen anything that looks quite like webOS. Between the card interface, the wave launcher, and gesture support (all of which I cover in the coming chapters), it's a *very* fresh take on how a phone should work — and I'm pretty sure you're going to like it! Check it out in Figure 1-3.

Figure 1-3: webOS and Pre put a fresh face on a phone interface.

Multitasking

As any iPhone owner can tell you, it's a bummer not being able to use multiple applications at the same time. Take Pandora Radio, for example, which is "on" in Figure 1-4). On the iPhone, you have to cut the music and exit the app if you want to check your e-mail, but with the Pre, the music just keeps on playing. On your Pre, you can run as many applications as you like at the same time, like you see in Figure 1-4. You're limited only by the amount of memory that the Pre has available, and don't worry — there's plenty of it, and it'll let you know if you're running out.

Synergy

Here's a problem you're probably all too familiar with. You have umpteen different instant messaging accounts and a bunch of e-mail inboxes, and you manage your contacts in three different places. The Synergy technology of webOS seeks to make managing all those tools a lot simpler by aggregating them into a single place. For example, say you have information about Joe Smith on Google Contacts, and you also know the same Joe Smith through Facebook. Your Pre can pull information from both sources into a single contact on the phone, and it won't duplicate the entries! It's got other tricks up its sleeve, too, like creating single threads of communication between you and others. In other words, if you talk to Joe on two IM accounts and you text message him a few times on top of that, it'll all appear on your Pre in a single window organized by time. Very cool.

Figure 1-4:
Look, ma, Pandora is still running!

Run more than one app at once.

Data freedom

Because your contacts, calendar, and application data are all silently and continuously synchronized to Palm's systems on the Internet, it's not a big deal if you lose your phone. (Well, it is, but hopefully not as *big* of a deal.) If that happens and you end up getting a new phone, just enter your Palm Profile login information to immediately get your critical information back right over the air. You can even remotely delete your old phone's memory, so that if your phone is truly lost or was stolen, no one will have access to your data.

Alerts

As important things happen on your Pre — meeting reminders occur, new e-mails, and so on — they collect at the bottom of the screen. That way, you can continue working without having to immediately acknowledge an alert. The alert icons keep hanging out at the bottom of the screen as a constant reminder that your phone is trying to tell you something important.

And that's just the beginning. Throughout this book, you'll learn more about all of these great webOS features and a whole lot more.

Plugging In with Your Palm Profile

Just like your e-mail address or your Google account, your Palm Profile helps define who you are in the digital world. When you turn on your Pre for the first time, it will ask you whether you already have a Palm Profile. If not, you'll create one on the spot because it's *just that important* for everything that the Pre does.

But what is a profile exactly?

If you owned a Palm from the old days, you probably remember the connecting your phone to a dock and pressing a button to synchronize your contacts, schedules, tasks, notes, and other goodies between what you'd changed on your computer that day with what you'd changed on your Palm. With the Pre, though, Palm decided that syncing by connecting your phone to a computer is way too much trouble. After all, your phone and your computer both have access to the same Internet, so what's the point in connecting them to exchange information when they can just communicate to the same services like Google, Exchange, and Facebook?

These kinds of Internet-based communal services are collectively known as "the cloud" — and not because they're white, puffy, and in the sky. (See Figure 1-5.) The term *cloud* is used as a metaphor for the Internet. Your data simply isn't all stored on one magical computer somewhere on the Internet (that'd be too easy!). But how do you get to all of it without tearing your hair out in the process? Put simply, your Palm Profile is what ties your information to you the cloud. You are you, no matter where you are or what you do.

As you add e-mail and calendar accounts, applications, and other information to your Pre, details are automatically saved to your Palm Profile. If you ever change to a different Pre or change to another kind of webOS phone (whatever that may be), you'll be able to instantly associate your Palm Profile to it and get back all your most important information right away. Gone are the days when losing your phone meant losing your contacts. As long as you have a Palm Profile, you can get back all your important info, no sweat.

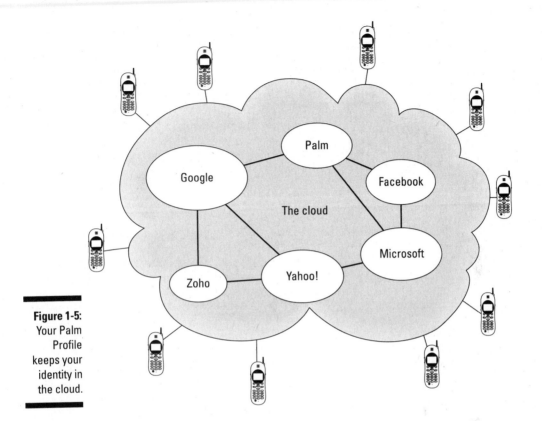

Figure 1-5:
Your Palm
Profile
keeps your
identity in
the cloud.

The Sky's the Limit . . .

The Pre is an incredibly powerful phone, and you'll find that you can do all sorts of stuff from the road that you may not have thought possible. You won't just be replying to text messages and e-mails — you'll be viewing Office documents, watching TV, finding your way when you get lost, browsing your favorite Web sites, and everything in between. There's even an application you can download that helps you run old Palm OS apps that you might have lying around!

The possibilities are limitless with webOS, and it's still a young platform. It'll be exciting to see what the Pre is going to be able to do as application developers stretch their imaginations and Palm rolls out updates over the coming months and years. And remember, any update that Palm makes will be automatically downloaded to your Pre with no hassle and no fuss. It doesn't get any easier than that.

. . . But It's Still a Limit

Is there anything your Pre can't do? If you purchased your Pre from Sprint in the United States or from Bell in Canada, that means you're using the CDMA version of the phone. CDMA is a wireless technology that isn't very common around the world, and you generally won't be able to take it overseas with you; it simply won't be able to make or receive calls or connect to the Internet.

Note: As of this writing, Verizon is also expected to release a CDMA version of the phone.

GSM is the far-more common type of wireless phone network around the world, used by carriers like AT&T, T-Mobile, Rogers, Vodafone, and countless others. If you purchased your Pre in Europe, that means that it's a GSM version, and you'll be able to use it pretty much anywhere although you won't have access to high-speed data services when you're in the United States or Canada because of the different radio frequencies that are used.

If you have a Sprint or Bell Pre, you might want to ask your network provider whether it has GSM phones available that you can take with you when you're leaving the country. Providers don't often advertise it, but typically, they can help you out so you still have access to a phone while you're globetrotting.

Chapter 2

Meeting and Greeting Your Pre

Your Palm Pre is capable of truly incredible things, and that's probably one of the reasons why you decided to buy it. Before you go launch down the path of mobile mega-productivity, though, take a minute or two to master a few tricks of the trade to get you off on the right foot. If you've used virtually any other cellphone, many of the concepts in this chapter will already be familiar, but some techniques are unique to webOS and Pre.

This chapter takes a look at the stuff your Pre is made of — the buttons, switches, gizmos, and doohickeys that you'll touch, press, move, and swipe (yup, I said "swipe") to use your phone. After that, you'll fire up the phone for the first time and set up your Palm Profile.

Your Pre at a Glance

Depending on any phone you've used, you might be used to hundreds (well, *seemingly* hundreds) of buttons on the face of the handset, the sides, the top, and everywhere in between. Palm's taken a starkly different tack with the Pre. Some buttons are still there, granted, but they're concealed extraordinarily well so as to make the phone look and feel like a totally solid, smooth pebble. Pretty, isn't it? Take a look at where all those buttons (and other notable physical features, for that matter) are hiding (see Figure 2-1).

Figure 2-1:
The Pre
from the
front, with
the slide
closed (left)
and open
(right).

Center button   Gesture area

Physical features

To the untrained eye, what you see in Figure 2-1 doesn't even look like a phone, does it? There's plenty of important stuff hiding here, though:

- **Touchscreen:** Your Pre is equipped with a display that runs at 320 x 480 resolution. Also known as "half VGA," this is the same resolution that the iPhone, T-Mobile G1, and BlackBerry Bold all use, so it's quickly becoming one of the de facto standard resolutions in the smartphone industry.

- **Earpiece:** I bet you know what this does! When you're using the Pre speakerphone, the sound comes from somewhere else, but I get to that in the next section.

↙ **Gesture area:** Unlike the iPhone and other touchscreen devices, the Pre has a special area *below* the screen that is also touch-sensitive — the *Gesture area*. This Gesture area is a concept that's unique to webOS, and it's important because you'll be using it regularly to navigate your Pre and to make things happen. Many actions on your Pre are controlled via gestures that you make onscreen with your fingertip, and some of those gestures either start in the gesture area or are contained completely within it. I talk about these gestures a lot in Chapter 3 and beyond.

↙ **Center button:** If you've used a device like a BlackBerry Pearl or a Curve, you might assume that this shiny ball is a trackball that you can roll with your thumb. Um, not quite! It's actually just a button, which you use to engage Card View. You'll find out more about Card View in Chapter 3.

↙ **Microphone:** This *is* a phone, after all, right?

↙ **Keyboard:** Slide open the phone, and *voilà!* This little wonder appears beneath the display. You use the keyboard for all your text entry on the Pre, as well as to perform a few special commands, such as Copy and Paste. I talk more about the keyboard and its special keys in the upcoming section, "The keyboard."

There isn't much you need to worry about on the sides of the Pre (as shown in Figure 2-2:

↙ **Volume:** Like with many phones, the Pre has two buttons on the side that you use to increase/decrease volume. Normally, this button adjusts ringer volume. When you're on a call, though, use the volume control to adjust call volume; likewise, when you're playing music, use the control to adjust music volume.

↙ **Micro-USB connector:** Use this port to charge your Pre and also to connect it to your computer to transfer music and photos. Although this connector port is typically covered with a small piece of plastic to protect it from dust and other environmental hazards that your phone is likely to encounter in the course of your daily travels, it's easily removed by prying it loose with your fingernail along the edge. And don't worry about losing it because it's tethered.

Figure 2-2:
The Pre
from the left
side (left)
and right
side (right).

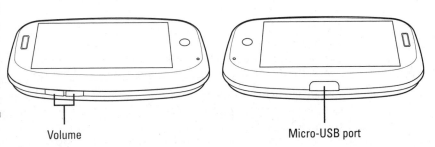

Volume   Micro-USB port

Half VGA

Half VGA uses an advanced form of touch sensitivity — *capacitive touch* — that improves upon the resistive touch technology used in older devices that requires far more pressure to operate.

Finally, take stock of the features along the Pre top and bottom edges (as shown in Figure 2-3), and also its the back:

- ✔ **Audio jack:** This is a standard 3.5mm headphone jack, which means that you can plug in almost any standard headphone. Plus, this jack is a three-pole jack, which means that you can also plug in wired hands-free headsets that include microphones for making calls. The Pre includes such a pair of ear buds, but if you're an audiophile, trust me when I tell you that you probably won't want to use them for listening to tunes.

- ✔ **Ringer switch:** If you've used an iPhone or a Palm Treo, this switch is a welcome feature that you're already acquainted with. To mute the Pre ringer and any alert sounds that the phone would otherwise make (such as an incoming text message), just slide the switch so that red is showing underneath. (Music and other media will still play, though.)

- ✔ **Power button:** Sure, the Power button's primary duty involves turning your phone on and off, but it's so much more! Okay, that might be an overstatement, but you *can* use it to sleep the display (which saves battery life and prevents things on the screen from accidentally being pressed) and wake it again while the phone is on.

- ✔ **Battery cover release:** This button allows you to pry off the rear cover of the phone, allowing you access to the battery. It's a little difficult to press, but that's intentional because you don't want the cover to come off unless you really mean it.

- ✔ **Speaker:** When you're using the Pre speakerphone capability or listening to music out loud (with or without your neighbor's permission), sound emanates from this speaker. And the rear of the phone is cleverly curved so that the speaker doesn't come in contact with the surface when it's set down, meaning that you don't have to worry about sound becoming quiet or muffled.

- ✔ **Camera:** The sensor and optics of your Pre 3.2 megapixel (MP) autofocus camera reside here.

- ✔ **Flash:** This tiny white spot is actually a powerful LED that can automatically light up to brighten dark scenes while you're trying to take a picture. It's not quite as effective as an actual flash like on a camera, but it's not bad in a pinch!

Speaker

Figure 2-3:
The Pre
from the top
(top), rear
(center),
and bottom
(bottom).

Audio
jack

The keyboard

Now take a closer look at the keyboard (see Figure 2-4). If you haven't yet done so, try sliding open your phone open to access the keyboard. This is how easy it is:

1. **Cradle the Pre in your hand, putting your thumb on the screen or immediately below it.**

2. **Push upward (that is, in the direction of the top edge of the phone).**

   It should slide open easily and stop when it's fully deployed.

Figure 2-4:
The
keyboard,
up close.

Shift

Orange key

Symbol

Enter

Palm Treo and Centro users will feel right at home with the layout, but regardless of what phone you're coming from, you'll find the Pre keyboard well designed and easy to use. Besides the typical QWERTY design, you'll notice a few special keys as well, as noted in Figure 2-4:

✔ **Orange:** Use the Orange key to access the smaller secondary numbers and symbols that appear in the upper corner of each key. For example, pressing Orange+A types an ampersand symbol (&).

✔ **Shift:** Just like any other keyboard, pressing Shift capitalizes letters.

- ✔ **Sym:** Use the Sym key (which stands for Symbol) primarily to access accented letters. For example, pressing A while holding down Sym brings up a menu from which you can select á, à, æ, and so on. You can also simply press Sym alone to bring up a full menu of available symbols, including math operators, fractions, currency markers, and more.

- ✔ **Enter:** Depending upon the application and the text field that you're using, press Enter to create a new line of text, or to submit your current entry (to a search engine, for example), like on a standard desktop computer keyboard.

Although you'll almost certainly find that you're most efficient on the keyboard when using two hands, Palm makes it possible to operate every function of the keyboard by using a single thumb. How, you ask? The secret is that the modifier keys — Orange, Shift, and Sym — can be used in multiple ways. The simplest method is to just hold down the modifier and the letter you want at the same time; to type a capital X, for example, simply hold down the Shift key and then press the X key. Small symbols appear below the text cursor to indicate when a modifier key has been enabled. See Figure 2-5.

Modifier key is enabled.

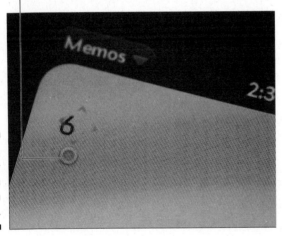

Figure 2-5:
A modifier key has been enabled.

If you're into using your Pre one-handed, though, this is where you'll want to pay close attention. By pressing Orange, Shift, or Sym briefly and then letting go, your Pre will know to wait for you to apply that modifier key to the next key you press. To type a capital X with the one-handed method, press Shift, let go, and then press X immediately afterward.

You have only about one-half second to press your next key after pressing Sym. Otherwise, the full menu of available symbols will appear.

Orange and Shift have one additional mode available: Lock. If you want to enter a string of capital letters, for example, you can enable Caps Lock (just like on a standard keyboard) by pressing Shift twice in a row. To disable Lock, just press the modifier key one more time.

Charging Your Pre Battery

You can read about all sorts of accessories you can use to keep your Pre's battery juiced up in Chapter 17, but there are no fewer than two different charging methods you'll find right in the box when you tear open the phone's packaging:

- **Using your computer:** Connect the included micro-USB cable between the micro-USB port on the side of your Pre and an available USB port on your computer to automatically start charging — a convenient option when you don't have an actual charger handy.

  Because computer USB ports don't provide a lot of electrical current, charging your Pre this way will take longer than connecting it to a wall outlet.

- **Using the wall charger:** Like with most rechargeable devices you own, the Pre includes a wall charger that plugs into a standard power outlet. The actual wall charger is just a small unit that connects to the outlet and has a USB port on the other side; simply connect the included micro-USB cable between the charger and your Pre's micro-USB port (as though you were charging it using your computer) and it'll start charging.

Turning On Your Pre the First Time

Enough looking at bits and pieces of the Pre hardware (for now, anyway). Time to dive in and take this baby for a spin. To start, press and hold the Power button (along the top-right edge of the phone) until the Palm logo appears on the display.

Setting up your Palm Profile

If you've been through Chapter 1, you already know that your Palm Profile is what ties your Pre to the world and keeps your data backed up. Your Profile is so important, in fact, that you can't even begin using your Pre until you configure your Profile on the phone. After your Pre finishes powering-on and you get past the Palm logo screen, you just need to go through a few quick steps to be on your way (and if you have to stop and turn off your phone in the middle of this process or you run out of battery, no worries — it'll pick right up where you left off next time):

1. **Choose the language that you wish to use (press your choice onscreen).**

   If you're using a Sprint Pre in the United States, your options are English and Spanish, but your choices might vary depending on where you're located and the operator that provided you with your Pre.

2. **Confirm your language selection by tapping the green button (it bears a check mark) on the screen.**

   If you make an error or want to change your mind, you can go back and make another selection by tapping the red button with the X in it.

   At this point, wait a moment for the phone to set your selected language; you'll see a spinning wheel while it does this. When it's done, you see the message `Phone Activated` onscreen.

3. **Tap the Next button.**

4. **After reading through the Terms & Conditions For Palm Services, tap the Accept button.**

   Only the strongest-willed among us will be able to brave the legalese of these terms and conditions, but if you wish to actually read through them in their entirety, you can do so by tapping the + button in the upper right of the screen to expand the document. After you're done, tap the – button to return to the Accept and Decline buttons.

At this point, you'll be looking at the Palm Profile setup screen (see Figure 2-6).

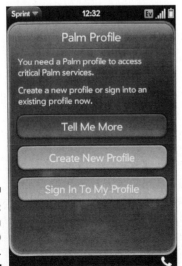

Figure 2-6:
The Palm
Profile setup
screen.

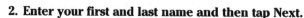

Restoring a Palm Profile

If you already have a Profile, tap Sign In to My Profile, enter your e-mail address and password, and then tap Sign In. Based on that information, your phone will automatically figure out who you are and restore your data and applications. So much for the pain of setting up a new phone, huh?

If you don't yet have a Palm Profile, don't worry; it's not too hard to set up. Starting at the Palm Profile setup screen

1. **Tap Create New Profile.**

2. **Enter your first and last name and then tap Next.**

   Your Pre will automatically capitalize your first and last name as you type — no need to hold down the Shift key.

3. **After you select a password, enter it, tap the Re-enter Password field, re-enter your password, and finally tap Next.**

   Be sure to choose a password that is both secure and something that you can remember. You'll need this password to restore your Palm Profile to another Pre (or a different webOS device altogether) or to remotely wipe your data if your phone is lost or stolen. Don't use your phone number, your birthday, your name, or anything that could be obvious to others!

4. **Enter your e-mail address and then tap Next.**

   You can also get to the next screen by pressing Enter on the keyboard.

   Just like the password that you selected, the e-mail address that you enter here should be an account that you will remember and have long-term access to.

   You briefly see a spinning wheel while Palm sets up your new Profile, after which you'll get a `Profile Created` message (see Figure 2-7).

5. **Tap Next.**

   In the screen that opens, you're given some information about location services, which allow applications (Maps, for example) to use features built in to your Pre to determine where you're located.

6. **Tap Next.**

Figure 2-7:
Congrat-
ulations!
Your Palm
Profile has
been suc-
cessfully
created.

7. **Read the Google Mobile Terms of Service, and then tap Agree.**

   Note the Allow Google's Location Service to Collect Anonymous and
   Aggregate Location Data check box (below the Terms of Service). This
   check box is selected by default. In a nutshell, checking this option helps
   Google make location information more accurate, which in turn helps
   you out because your phone can identify your location more precisely.
   It's up to you whether you want to allow this, but there's no real
   advantage to unchecking it.

   Technically, you can tap the Don't Agree button on this screen if you
   don't want to agree to Google's terms of service, but I don't recommend
   it. If you do this, software won't have access to your location information,
   which makes some applications less useful (or, in some cases, totally
   useless).

8. **(Optional) To enable Auto Locate, tap Enable Auto Locate; otherwise,
   tap Ask Each Time.**

   If the Auto Locate feature is disabled, you will be asked for permission
   every time an application on your Pre asks to know where you are. If
   you're worried about privacy, you can tap Ask Each Time here to make
   sure that you're made aware whenever an application tries to get this
   information. For maximum convenience and to keep distractions to a
   minimum, I recommend that you enable this feature, but this choice is
   entirely yours.

Finally, you'll be given a quick interactive tour on some finger gestures that will help you navigate through your Pre. (Don't worry if you need some more practice with these because these gestures are covered thoroughly in Chapter 3.) The phone will then restart to finish configuring your Profile. When that process is complete, you'll be ready to go!

I know you want to dig right in, but before you start exploring your fully configured, fully functional Pre, there's one more thing you'll want to do: Return to your computer and open the e-mail account that you entered on the phone while setting up your Palm Profile. You should find that you received an e-mail from Palm asking you to confirm the address you entered by clicking a link and filling out some details. Run through this, choose a security question, and answer (choose both carefully because they'll bail you out in case you ever forget your Palm Profile password), and then click Submit. See, that was easy, wasn't it?

Locking Your Phone

No, I'm not talking about putting your phone inside a safe. Your Pre has a few different ways that it can protect itself against accidental key presses and unwanted intruders.

Standard unlock

First off, the standard lock screen (as shown in Figure 2-8) appears when the screen is turned on after it's been off for more than about a minute. This screen prevents you from accidentally entering keystrokes or screen taps while the phone is in your pocket or somewhere else where it might brush up against objects. This is similar to the keyguard feature found on many other phones.

To unlock your phone from the lock screen, place your finger on the gold ball at the bottom and drag it anywhere above the white curved line that appears. Then let go. The Pre will be unlocked, and you're returned to the screen where you left off the last time the screen turned off.

Secure unlock

If you want to kick up the security a notch or two, you can require either a four-digit PIN (just like the ATM at the bank) or a password to unlock and use the phone after the screen has been turned off. To configure this

1. **Open Launcher.**

   See Chapter 3 for more details on Launcher and opening applications.

Figure 2-8:
The lock
screen.

2. **Tap the icon for Screen & Lock.**

   Unless you moved it to another location, you'll find Screen & Lock on
   the third page of Launcher applications. To get to it, swipe twice on the
   screen, moving your finger from right to left.

   You're presented with the Screen & Lock preferences screen, as shown
   in Figure 2-9.

Figure 2-9:
The Screen
& Lock
preferences
screen.

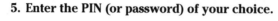
3. **Scroll down to the bottom of the screen and tap the button below the section labeled Secure Unlock.**

   By default, this button is labeled Off.

   You're presented with three options:

   - Off
   - Simple PIN
   - Password

4. **Tap the secure unlock type you wish to use.**

5. **Enter the PIN (or password) of your choice.**

   Be sure to select something you can remember (but will be difficult for others to guess).

   - *If you select a PIN,* another screen will appear, where you're asked to enter your PIN again.

   - *If you select a password,* you need to enter it twice in the provided fields.

6. **If you're entering a password, tap the Done button after you enter and confirm your password in the provided fields.**

   You're returned to the Screen & Lock preferences screen, and your secure unlock selection will be indicated where the Off button used to be. To change the secure unlock type (or to change it back to Off again), press this button. You'll to enter need your PIN or password to change this option.

After setting up secure unlock, you'll be prompted for your PIN or password every time you turn on your Pre's screen — a comforting feature when you have some e-mails on there that you'd rather prying eyes not see.

Chapter 3

Getting Around Your Pre

- -

- -

*W*ith your Pre fully charged (see Chapter 2 for details on how to get that accomplished, by the way), your Palm Profile set up (also in Chapter 2), your shoelaces tied, and your seatbelt firmly fastened, what's next? At this point, it's time to master how to navigate all the nooks and crannies that make up the many parts of webOS. For new users, this is usually the part where you'll experience your fair share of "oohs" and "aahs" as you see your Pre do things that you've never, ever seen a phone do before.

Even for users of older Palm devices running Palm OS or Windows Mobile, this is a really critical chapter because you'll find that a lot has changed. When Palm created webOS, it thoroughly rethought even the most fundamental aspects of how a phone should work. The result is a clean, elegant, easy-to-use interface that you'll absolutely love. There is a bit of a learning curve, and my goal here is to make that curve as gentle of a slope as possible.

In this chapter, you'll see how to open applications and navigate between them, find out the difference between the Quick Launch toolbar and an "activity card," and discover how to control almost everything your Pre can do with just a few swipes of your finger.

Gestures: Let Your Fingers Do the Walking

Throughout this book, you'll hear me refer to *gestures* pretty frequently. Why's that? Like the iPhone, the Palm Pre uses finger motions to get some things done. Actually, the Pre goes beyond the iPhone in terms of the sheer number of tasks you can accomplish using gestures alone. Here's a comprehensive list of the gestures you'll use and what they're used for:

- **Center button:** This one isn't a gesture, per se, but I'm including it here anyway because you'll use it frequently and it involves your finger. Pressing the shiny ball below the black Gesture area that resides below the Pre's screen will return you to Card View, no matter where you are in the Pre, what you're doing, or what application you're using. You can see the Center button and the Gesture area in Figure 3-1.

Figure 3-1:
The Center button and Gesture area.

Center button   Gesture area

✔ **Tap:** A quick tap of your fingertip on the screen is used primarily for two things:

- *Triggering actions:* You tap icons in Launcher to open applications, tap buttons to perform whatever function is listed on the text on the button, and tap menus to open them.

- *Selecting things:* You tap pictures to select them (when choosing a picture for a contact, for example — see Chapter 8 for details) and tap text to place your cursor there so you can type.

✔ **Swipe on screen:** A *swipe* occurs when you place your finger on one side of the screen and move it in one fluid motion to the opposite side.

When you swipe from left to right or from right to left, this gesture is used for a few things:

- *Moving between items:* You can move between cards in Card View or photos in the Photos application using left-to-right and right-to-left swipe gestures.

- *Scrolling:* You can move through a Web page by swiping your finger up or down.

- *Deleting items:* When you have a list of items on the Pre (in your Email inbox, for example), you can often delete individual items by swiping from left to right or from right to left.

Swiping from top to bottom or from bottom to top is most frequently used for scrolling — for example, in the Web application — but you will also occasionally use it for other things, like opening Launcher by swiping upward from the Quick Launch toolbar, as shown in the figure here (and more about this later in the chapter).

✔ **Back:** Swiping your finger from right to left in the black Gesture area below the screen is a *back gesture*. As its name implies, it simply returns you to wherever you were last. For example, if you select a category of photos in the Photos application, you can get back to the category list using the back gesture; in the Web application, the back gesture goes back to the last page you were browsing.

✔ **Quick Launch:** There's a special gesture just for showing the Quick Launch toolbar from anywhere in the Pre, which you'll read about later in this chapter. Hold your finger down in the black Gesture area and drag it upward onto the screen; you'll notice a curvy version of the Quick Launch toolbar is visible. Without taking your finger off the screen, select the application you want to launch. Then lift your finger off the screen and the application launches.

✔ **Flick:** The *flick gesture* is similar to a swipe, but much faster! Flicks are used in a couple ways:

- *Scrolling long distances:* In lists of items (like your Email inbox) and Web pages, flicking your finger in any direction will scroll a long distance in that direction. That way, you don't need to hold your finger down and keep swiping over and over again to get to where you're going. Try this gesture out a few times. You'll get the hang of it pretty quickly.

- *Closing an open application:* By flicking a card upward in Card View, the application represented by that card will close. You'll find out more about this later in this chapter.

The Web application is a great place to practice flicking, and to better understand the difference between swiping and flicking. Just open a Web page and start trying gestures to get a feel for how the scrolling happens.

✔ **Hold:** When you press your fingertip on the screen and hold it there, this stops a list or Web page from scrolling after it's been started with a flick gesture. This scrolling decelerates over time and will eventually stop on its own, but if you want to stop it right now, just hold your finger on the screen. You'll also hold your finger on the screen to "pick up" cards in Card View and icons in Launcher so that they can be moved to other locations. You'll find out all about this later in the chapter.

✔ **Drag:** Dragging occurs when you have something selected on the screen by holding it (using the gesture I just described), and you move your finger on the screen without lifting it. This will actually move an object, like a card in Card View or an icon in Launcher.

✔ **Pinch:** Anyone familiar with the iPhone will recognize this particular gesture quite well! Pinching occurs when you place two fingertips on the screen (as shown in Figure 3-2) and move them toward each other or away from each other. When you move them toward each other, this zooms out (a photo in Photos, or a Web page in Web, for instance) — that is, everything gets smaller. Conversely, moving your fingers away from each other zooms in so everything gets bigger.

Figure 3-2:
Pinch to
zoom in.

Opening Applications with Quick Launch and Launcher

As their names imply, Launcher and Quick Launch are the two major ways you launch applications on your Pre. The Quick Launch toolbar is where you'll put your most frequently used apps. For many users, the default choices are the Dialer, Contacts, Email, and Calendar. Launcher is where everything else goes.

As their names imply, Launcher and Quick Launch are the two major ways you launch applications on your Pre:

- ✔ **Quick Launch toolbar:** Here you can place up to five icons for your most frequently used apps for quick and easy access. The Launcher icon (on the far right) is a default: You can't alter that. Many users opt for the Dialer, Contacts, Email, and Calendar.

- ✔ **Launcher:** This is the repository — the big "folder," if you will — of all your apps and settings preferences.

Here's how they work together.

1. **You call up the Quick Launch toolbar by pressing the Center button to open Card View.**

   (You can also call up the toolbar when you have an app open full-screen; I talk about that in a bit.)

2. **Then you open Launcher by tapping that icon on the toolbar.**

The Quick Launch toolbar

Just like almost everything on the Pre, the little Quick Launch toolbar does more than you might think. It's way more than just a pretty strip of icons at the bottom of the screen!

Using Quick Launch anywhere

In Card View, you always see the Quick Launch toolbar, but you can also call it up when you have an application taking up the entire screen. That means that you can easily launch your most frequently used applications without going all the way into Launcher and finding what you need. Sweet.

In Figure 3-3, I'm calling up the Quick Launch toolbar while using the phone dial pad. Note that you can see the Quick Launch toolbar's Calendar and Launcher icons on top of the dial pad.

Figure 3-3:
Calling up the Quick Launch toolbar.

1. **Press and hold your finger in the Gesture area.**

   The Gesture area is that black area below the Pre screen.

2. **Drag your finger upward onto the screen.**

   As you do this, the most magical thing will happen: A wavy version of the Quick Launch toolbar appears as if you've charmed a snake from a basket. The area of the toolbar directly above your finger is raised upward, and the name of the application closest to your finger appears directly above the icon. This indicates the selected icon.

3. **After you select the icon of the application you want to launch, let go: that is, take your finger off the screen.**

   And that's it! The selected application immediately launches.

The application you're in won't close: It's still accessible from Card View. If you want to close it, go to Card View and flick the card upward off the screen.

Reorganizing the Quick Launch toolbar

As mentioned earlier in the chapter, the Launcher icon on the Quick Launch toolbar is permanently affixed on the right side (nope, it can't be moved or deleted), but the rest of the bar is totally yours to customize.

To rearrange icons, you'll need to be in a place where the Quick Launch toolbar stays visible without bringing it up using the Gesture area. Card View and Launcher both work perfectly for this.

To move an icon on the Quick Launch toolbar

1. **Press and hold your finger on the icon you wish to move.**

   After about one-half second, a white halo appears around the icon, indicating that it can now be moved.

2. **Without lifting your finger from the screen, move your finger to the location on the Quick Launch toolbar where you want the icon to reside.**

   The other icons on the bar automatically move to make room for you. (Awfully courteous of them!)

3. **Drop (and place) the icon by lifting your finger off the screen.**

To add or remove icons from the Quick Launch toolbar, you must be in Launcher because that's your central warehouse where all icons are stored. When you remove an icon from the toolbar, it's returned to a Launcher page. Similarly, adding an icon to the bar removes it from its location in the Launcher. In other words, icons can only be in one place at any given time.

The Quick Launch toolbar can have a maximum of five icons, and one is permanently taken up by Launcher. Do the math to figure out that leaves you four locations to play with.

Say you're trying to forget some silly work-related meetings, so you want to replace the Calendar application with the Music application (a good choice, if you ask me). First, you have to remove Calendar:

1. **Open Launcher (tap the Launcher icon on the Quick Launch toolbar).**

2. **Press and hold your finger on the Calendar icon.**

   By now, you probably know the drill. The icon sports a white halo after about one-half second to let you know that it can now be moved.

3. **Without removing your finger from the screen, move the icon to Launcher.**

   Just like when you're reorganizing icons within Launcher, you can place the Calendar icon wherever you like and on any page.

4. **Lift your finger off the screen when the Calendar icon is where you want it to be.**

Next, add the new icon (in this example, Music) to the Quick Launch toolbar by basically performing the preceding steps but in reverse:

1. **Press and hold your finger on the Music icon in Launcher until its white halo appears.**

2. **Move the icon to a location of your choosing on the Quick Launch toolbar.**

   Assuming you have fewer than five icons on the Quick Launch bar right now (which you should at this point), they'll automatically move to accommodate you.

3. **Lift your finger off the screen.**

   Congratulations! You just customized your Quick Launch toolbar.

Launcher basics

Launcher is like the Start menu on a Windows PC or the Applications folder of a Mac: the home base where the icons for all your applications and settings pages live. As you install new applications on your Pre (more on that in Chapter 15), their icons automatically appear here. Similarly, when you remove an application, its icon automatically disappears.

Unlike typical applications, though, Launcher can't be made into a card. Instead, when you press the Center button to get to Card View, Launcher simply slides toward the bottom of the screen and goes away. It's never too far, though — you can always access it by going to the Quick Launch toolbar and selecting its icon.

As you might imagine, Launcher is important. It's so important, in fact, that Palm has dedicated a spot for it on the Quick Launch toolbar. And unlike other icons on the toolbar, Launcher can't be moved or deleted. To access it

1. **Open the Quick Launch toolbar by pressing the Center button to return to Card View.**

   The Quick Launch toolbar appears at the bottom of the screen in Card View. In the previous section, read about how to open the Quick Launch bar while in any application on the Pre.

2. **Tap the Launcher icon, as shown here.**

   The icon always appears on the far right of the Quick Launch toolbar.

Launcher

Alternatively, you can access Launcher by going to Card View and flicking your finger upward from the Quick Launch toolbar to the area of the screen above it.

Browsing and opening applications

Launcher is divided into three pages, which can be used to organize your applications however you like. You move between these pages much the same way that you move between cards: Hold down your finger anywhere in the gray area of the Launcher (even if it's on an icon, that's okay) and simply flick it left to move right one page or flick it right to move left one page.

What you see in Figure 3-4 shows one of the three pages; you can't see them all at once.

Application icons

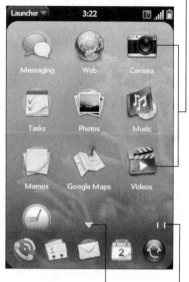

Figure 3-4:
The
Launcher.

Scroll down indicator

Current Launcher page indicator

 At the bottom of Launcher, just above the Quick Launch toolbar, you can find an indication of what Launcher page you're viewing. When you see two small vertical bars on the right side of the screen (as shown in Figure 3-4), that means you're on the leftmost page. When you see one bar on the left side of the screen and one on the right, you're on the middle page. And (go figure), two bars on the left indicates that you're on the rightmost page.

If there are more icons than can fit onscreen at once, each page can be scrolled up and down: Hold your finger anywhere within Launcher and move your finger up or down. If there are more icons above or below the visible area of a page, arrows appear near the top or bottom of the screen to indicate where you need to scroll to see the hidden stuff.

When you find the icon of the application you wish to launch, just press it briefly with your finger.

Organizing applications

By default, applications that you install appear in the first page of Launcher and settings appear in the third, but you're welcome to reorganize these however you like. The process is similar to reordering cards in Card View. To move an icon in Launcher

1. **Press and hold your finger on the icon you wish to move.**

   After about a half second, a white halo appears around the icon you're pressing. After the halo appears, it can be moved.

2. **Without lifting your finger from the screen, move the icon to the position you like.**

   While you move this icon over other icons, Launcher automatically makes room for you. If you want to move the icon to an area or a page that isn't visible, that's not a problem. Change pages by moving your finger near the left or right edge of the screen, and you can move up or down in the current page by moving your finger to the top or bottom edge.

   If you have trouble with this on the first try, don't give up — just hold the icon again and start again. You'll have it down pat after a few tries.

3. **Drop the icon in its new location by taking your finger off the screen.**

Closing Launcher

Launcher automatically closes when you open an application from it. To make the Launcher go away without opening an application, tap the Launcher icon in the lower right of the screen on the Quick Launch toolbar, or you can press the Center button.

Card View: A Bird's-Eye View of Your Open Applications

Each and every time you turn on your Pre, the first thing you'll see (after the Palm logo, that is) Card View (see Figure 3-5). The closest equivalent to the Card View on other phones is the home screen. Think of Card View as your Pre's home base, the place that you'll be coming back to time after time when you're not making calls or using applications.

To get to Card View at any time, just press the Center button in the Gesture area below the Pre screen. This works regardless of what application you're using.

The lay of the land

When you first start your Pre, you don't have any applications open, but Palm calls this view Card View because each open application is roughly the shape of a card — which makes them easy to see and manage. Don't worry, though; I get to application management in Card View in the next section. For now, peruse Figure 3-5 for a look at some of the important items on the screen.

Background   Status bar

Figure 3-5:
Card view.

Dashboard

Quick Launch toolbar

✔ **Status bar:** This black bar at the top of the screen is visible from almost anywhere on your Pre although certain applications might choose to hide it (video players, for example, to maximize the size of the video that you can see). Quite a few things can show up in the status bar depending on where you are and what you're doing. I cover some of these as I discuss them, but for now, here are the major ones that you're likely to see when you first turn on the phone:

• *Network name or menu:* In Card View or when the Pre is locked (read about locking in Chapter 2), the network that your phone is using is displayed here. If you're using a Pre from Sprint in the United States, for example, you see Sprint here. If you're using an application, you see that application's menu in place of the network name. (Menus are covered later in this chapter.)

• *Time:* The current time. Unless you changed settings on your Pre, this time is automatically updated as you travel between time zones (which means you have one less excuse for being late to that 8 a.m. meeting). If the phone is locked, this area shows the current date instead because the time is already displayed in much larger text below the status bar.

- *Data icon:* If your Pre is in an area served by a data network, you see an icon here indicating the type of network available: 1x for a 1xRTT network, or Ev for a faster EV-DO network. Normally, this icon has a light gray background with black text, but if the phone is transferring data and actively using the data connection — when you're browsing the Web, using Maps, or synchronizing your e-mail, for example — it'll change to a dark gray background with light gray text.

- *Signal strength indicator:* This indicator shows you how strong your network reception is, on a scale of zero to five bars. Generally speaking, higher signal strength means that callers will "break up" less, you'll have a lower chance of dropping calls, and data services (like Web browsing) will run faster.

- *Battery strength indicator:* The amount of remaining battery life is indicated as a filled green area inside a battery icon. The green area becomes shorter as your battery depletes, and when you get close to running out of juice, it'll change from green to red. Time for a charge! — see Chapter 2 for a refresher on how to make that happen.

When you touch the time, data icon, signal strength indicator, or battery strength indicator in the status bar, you get a pop-up window in the upper-right corner of the screen that shows the day and date; the remaining battery charge (expressed as a percentage); and options to enable or disable Wi-Fi, Bluetooth, and Airplane Mode. This is especially handy if you want to see precisely how much battery life you have left before you need to plug in for a charge.

✔ **Background:** This area is often covered with a smattering of activity cards (more on those when applications are discussed later in the next section). Out of the gate, though, all you see is your wallpaper. If you don't want the default wallpaper, there's a setting to change it. See the section, "Changing your Card View background," later in this chapter for details on how to do that.

✔ **Quick Launch toolbar:** Windows users will likely be well acquainted with this feature, which works much the same in Windows. The Quick Launch toolbar is simply a quick way to access commonly used applications. Attention Mac users: Think of this as the Dock. I explore the Quick Launch toolbar earlier in this chapter; it has some neat tricks up its sleeve.

✔ **Dashboard:** This area shows your *notifications,* which are alerts that your Pre and your various applications want you to be aware of. They can be anything — reminders for appointments, unread e-mail, a music track that's playing — the sky's the limit.

Alphabet soup: CDMA, 1xRTT, and EV-DO

Around the world, network operators employ a number of technology standards in their wireless networks, which means that only certain phones can be used with certain operators and in certain countries. If you purchased your Pre from Sprint in the United States or from Bell in Canada, your Pre uses CDMA (Code Division Multiple Access) technology. In addition to the United States and Canada, CDMA phones can be used in parts of Latin America and Asia, but not in Europe. (Your operator can provide you with a full list of countries where your Pre will work and inform you what to do if you need to travel to a country where it won't.)

CDMA networks predominantly use two technologies to transfer data to and from your phone. The older of these technologies is 1xRTT (1 times Radio Transmission Technology), which is limited to 144 kilobits per second — probably less than ten percent of your home Internet connection! The newer technology — EV-DO (Evolution-Data Optimized) — is capable of transferring several megabits per second worth of information to your phone. Obviously, fast is good. And, fortunately, Sprint has rolled out EV-DO over a very large portion of its network, so you should very rarely see the 1x icon in the status bar of your Pre.

Activity cards

You can open applications on the Pre much like you have applications running on your Mac or PC; check out "Launcher basics" earlier in the chapter to see how to open applications. But what do they look like when they're open? In Chapter 2, I mention how pressing the Center button below the screen returns you to Card View from wherever you are in the operating system. Think of it like using the Show Desktop command in Windows, or Exposé on a Mac. It's a quick way to find your way back home and get a glance at all the applications running on your Pre.

On a Pre, open applications take the form of *activity cards* (see Figure 3-6), which are more generally just called *cards* (and that's how I refer to them throughout the remainder of this book). A card is simply a miniaturized view of an application that sits inside Card View. Each card you see represents an open application. As you open applications, new cards are created in a horizontal line from left to right, but they can be reordered if you like — more on that later in the chapter.

You think that's cool? You haven't seen anything yet: These cards are actually *live!* They work and respond just as though you were using the application on the full screen! They update to show new information as it arrives (this would be handy for a weather app, for example), and certain applications like Web even rotate to stay right-side up when you rotate your phone.

Activity cards

Figure 3-6:
Card View,
filled with
activity
cards.
The Email
application
is in the
center.

If you've used an iPhone, you understand why functionality like Card View is so helpful. And if you haven't used an iPhone, here's why Card View rocks: No longer are you limited having only one application open at a time. No longer is the only way to get to another application is to close the one that you're using. Nope, Card View is magical because it allows you to keep more than one app open at a time. That means that you can always have your most frequently used applications — Contacts, Calendar, and Email, for example — just one click away. And because the cards are live, you can see what's going on in each of the apps with a couple swipes of the finger across the display.

Here's a minor caveat, though, to keep in mind when you run more than one app at a time. Because each card represents an open application, each and every card is consuming the phone's battery power, processor power, and memory! Even though the Pre is an incredibly powerful phone with lots of these precious resources to go around, I recommend closing applications when you're not using them; see the upcoming section "Closing cards." You'll save resources, and you'll help reduce clutter in Card View. And, if you do have too many cards open and your phone starts to buckle under the load, your Pre will warn you that it's time to close some.

Moving your finger onscreen to cause an action to occur on your Pre is a *gesture.* Throughout this chapter and the book, I tell you about some great gestures that you'll be using. For now, though, keep reading to see some of the basic gestures that you can use to manage Card View.

Moving between cards and maximizing cards

Managing cards is a breeze. While in Card View, all open cards appear in a horizontal row, spanning left to right.

1. **Place and hold your finger (I usually use my thumb, but the choice is yours) on the screen so that it's touching a card.**

2. **Move your finger left or right.**

You don't need to keep your finger on the screen until the next card is showing. You can also flick your finger in either direction so that it just glances off the screen momentarily. It sounds like a minor difference, but you'll probably find that it's a much more natural motion in practice.

One card — the active card — is always centered on the screen. You can see an example of this in Figure 3-6. Press once on this card to maximize that application so that it fills your screen; when an app is maximized like this, you can use it and interact with it. Although applications can show information in Card View, you still need to view them full-screen to actually use them. Otherwise, there's just not enough space on the card itself (and if you disagree, congratulations — you have incredible eyesight!).

Closing cards

As mentioned earlier, I recommend closing cards that you're not using. Not only does it help your Pre devote more memory and processor power to other applications and last longer on a battery charge, but keeping your screen tidy leaves Card View uncluttered so that you can easily find what you're looking for.

Even though closing cards means you're closing the application itself, don't worry about your data — you'll never lose it. Whenever you close a card, applications know to automatically save anything you're working on so they where you left off the next time you open it.

Fortunately, closing cards is one of the most amusing things you can do on the Pre; I can't put my finger on why (pun intended), but for some reason, it's a really satisfying experience, and it's often the thing that widens folks' eyes when they see the Pre in action for the very first time.

In a nutshell, to close a card, you go to Card View and "throw" it off the screen (see Figure 3-7). *Note:* You can't close a card when the application is full screen.

1. **Press and hold your finger on the card that you want to close.**

2. **Flick it upward so it flies off the screen.**

The card disappears, and the remaining open cards move together to fill the gap you just created. Wasn't that cool?

Figure 3-7:
Closing a
card.

To get to Card View at any time, just press the Center button in the Gesture area below the Pre screen. This works regardless of what application you're using.

Rearranging cards

If you want to see your cards in a particular order (see Figure 3-8), that's no problem:

1. **Press and hold down a card.**

   After about half a second, the card becomes semi-transparent, and all open cards zoom out (that is, become smaller on the screen) so that you can see more of them onscreen at once.

2. **Move the card under your finger to the left or right so that it's between the cards you want.**

   As you move the card, gaps are automatically created between other open cards so that it's easier to position. In Figure 3-8, I'm moving the phone dial pad application card to a different location in the line.

3. **Let go of the card by taking your finger off the screen.**

4. **Tap the background of Card View (that is, your wallpaper) to zoom the cards back to their normal size.**

   You can also go directly into an application so that it's taking up the full screen by pressing on a card while zoomed out — the cards work just as they normally would.

Figure 3-8:
Move a
card to a
different
location.

Changing your Card View background

Maybe you're sick of the default background on your Pre (if you're not, that's ok too). Here's how to change the wallpaper you see in the background behind Card View.

1. **Open Launcher.**

   See the section "Launcher basics" earlier in this chapter for more details on Launcher and how to use it.

2. **Tap the icon for Screen & Lock.**

   Unless you moved it, this is located on the third page of Launcher icons.

   The Screen & Lock preferences screen appears.

3. **Tap the Change Wallpaper button.**

   A new screen appears with all the folders of photos that are available on your Pre. These are the same groupings that you'll find in the Photos application, which I describe in detail in Chapter 11.

4. **Tap the folder you want to browse and then tap the image you want to use as your wallpaper, or tap the New Photo button at the top of the screen if you want to take a new picture right now using the Pre camera.**

   Using the camera is described in Chapter 11.

   The picture you selected (or just took) will be shown full-screen.

5. **Zoom in and out using pinch gestures (described earlier in this chapter) and pan around the image by dragging your finger on the screen. The visible area of the selected image will be used as the wallpaper.**

6. **When you're happy with your selection, tap the Set Wallpaper button at the top of the screen.**

   You return to the Screen & Lock preferences screen. The next time you go to Card View, you'll see your new wallpaper in action!

Part II
All About Communicating

It's an e-mail from my mother. She wants me to know how happy she is for us.

In this part . . .

Modern smartphones like the Pre are really blurring the lines between portable computers, personal digital assistants, and phones, and those lines get blurrier seemingly each and every day. Ultimately, though, you need your phone to communicate whether you're using a Pre or one of those big brick phones from the 1980s — and communicating is what Part II is all about.

I start things off in Chapter 4 the old-fashioned way — making voice calls and text messages — and from there you'll move on to e-mail in Chapter 5 and instant messaging in Chapter 6. If it's possible to be "over-connected," the Pre will certainly get you there in a hurry — and I'm going to help you!

Chapter 4

Making and Receiving Calls and Text Messages

In This Chapter

▶ Making and receiving calls

▶ What you can do while you're on the phone

▶ Working with voice mail

▶ Text messaging

With all its extra features and functionality and organizing tools, don't forget that your Pre is a phone, after all. Besides all the other cool things you can do with it, its primary job is to allow you to make and receive phone calls and send and receive text messages. In this chapter, you'll explore the phone features of your Pre.

Making Calls

Making a call from your Pre is pretty darned simple. And because folks are different, Pre offers a number of ways to quickly reach out and touch someone. Here are some ways to initiate calls on your Pre, all of which I talk about in more detail in the upcoming sections:

✔ Using the phone dial pad

✔ From Launcher or in Card View

✔ By contact name

✔ Using speed dial

✔ Redialing the last number called

✔ Using a number that appears on a Web page or in an e-mail or text message

Using the phone dial pad

To access the phone portion of your Pre, just tap the Phone icon on the Quick Launch toolbar at the bottom of the Pre main screen.

Phone

Your Pre displays the phone dial pad shown in Figure 4-1.

Battery

Signal strength | Contact icon

Figure 4-1:
The Pre's
phone
dialing pad.

Voicemail   Call History

Then, to dial the number, simply tap each digit, on the dial pad. If you make an error and tap an incorrect number, use the Backspace button that appears to the right of the number to erase it (see Figure 4-2).

Backspace button

Figure 4-2:
Tap the
Backspace
button on
the dial pad
to erase an
incorrect
number.

Tap to dial the call.

After you finish entering the number, tap the green phone icon below the dial pad to connect the call.

While you're talking, the phone icon turns orange. When you finish talking, press the orange phone icon to end the call.

Dialing from Launcher or Card View

If you prefer, you can bypass using the dial pad shown in Figure 4-1. Instead, from either Launcher or in Card View, you can simply type the number using the Pre keyboard.

When you dial from the keyboard, you don't need to press and hold the Orange key. As you press the keys, the Pre performs a universal search, and the phone number appears at the top of the screen. If the number you type isn't associated with an existing contact, the Pre gives you the option to add the number to your Contacts, as shown in the left screen of Figure 4-3. If you type in a number associated with a contact, the contact's name appears, as shown in the right screen of Figure 4-3.

Figure 4-3:
When
you dial
a number
associated
with a
contact, the
Universal
Search
feature
displays the
contact's
name.

Then, to dial the number, tap the phone icon beside the number. You can also press the Enter key on the keypad to dial the number.

You can access Card View while viewing any maximized app if you press the phone's Center button (located below the screen). The Pre will reduce the size of all open apps to cards, and you'll see the phone's main screen behind the cards.

Using contact information

You'll take a closer look at everything contacts can do in Chapter 8, but for now, see how you can use them to make calls. In conjunction with the Pre Universal Search feature that I cover in Chapter 7, you can use information stored for a contact to call the contact in a number of ways:

✔ From Launcher or Card View
✔ From the phone dial pad
✔ From Contacts

From Launcher or Card View, you can use the Pre keyboard to type a name stored in Contacts. Your Pre searches for the name among your contacts and displays any matches it finds (see Figure 4-4).

Figure 4-4:
Using a
contact's
name to
search.

When you see the contact you want, tap the phone number shown. Pre switches to the phone dial pad and dials the number for you (see Figure 4-5). This method is a little different from Pre speed dialing, which I cover shortly.

Contact icon

Figure 4-5:
Dial a phone
number
obtained via
Contacts.

Using speed dial

If you assign a speed dial number to a contact, you can use it to place a call to the contact. Of course, you need to have entered some contact names and numbers first. (See Chapter 8 for how.) To assign a speed dial number to a contact, follow these steps:

1. **Tap the Contacts icon on the Quick Launch toolbar.**

2. **Find and tap the contact's name.**

3. **Tap the Contacts application menu; from the menu that appears, tap Set Speed Dial.**

4. **In the screen that appears, tap the phone number to which you want to assign a speed dial character.**

5. **Tap the letter or number/letter key you want to use as a speed dial character (see Figure 4-6).**

   You can scroll to view all your choices.

Choose the speed dial key.

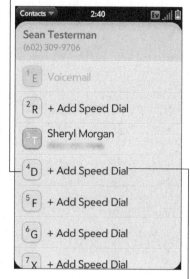

Figure 4-6: Select a phone number to which to assign a speed dial character.

Then tap this.

The contact's record redisplays, and the keyboard letter you selected appears beside the phone number (see Figure 4-7).

Speed dial icon

Figure 4-7:
A contact
with an
assigned
speed dial.

To use a speed dial to call a contact, display Launcher, Card View, or the phone dial pad. Then, press and hold the speed dial key you assigned to the contact's phone number. Your Pre will initiate the call.

Redialing the last number called

Another way to initiate a call is to just redial the last number you called. Display the phone's dial pad, and press the green phone icon below the dial pad. The last number you called appears at the top of the dial pad. Tap the green phone icon below the dial pad again, and your Pre makes the call.

Dialing a number from a Web page or message

Your Pre is smart enough to recognize most phone numbers that appear as links on Web pages or in e-mail, text, or multimedia messages. For example, on the left of Figure 4-8, you see the phone number listed on the Best Buy Web site.

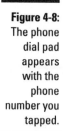

Figure 4-8:
The phone
dial pad
appears
with the
phone
number you
tapped.

When you tap the number, the Pre phone dial pad appears with the number already entered, as shown on the right side of Figure 4-8. To dial the number, tap the green phone icon below the dial pad.

Using dialing shortcuts

You can set up dialing shortcuts so that your Pre adds a prefix to numbers you dial frequently. Suppose, for example, that your company's phone system assigns 11 numbers to each extension, such as 1-999-555-1234. But, when you dial a number using a phone that's part of the company's system, you only need to dial the last four digits: 1234 in this example.

You can create a dialing shortcut for your company's extensions on your Pre where you only dial the last four digits of a company extension on your Pre, and the Pre will add the required preceding digits to the number when the Pre dials.

To create a dialing shortcut like the one described in this section, follow these steps:

1. **On the Quick Launch toolbar, tap the Phone icon to launch the phone dial pad.**

2. **Tap the menu with your network name at the top of the phone dialing pad. On the menu that appears, tap Preferences.**

   The Phone Preferences screen appears (see Figure 4-9).

Figure 4-9:
The Phone
Preferences
screen.

3. **Tap Add New Number, in the Dialing Shortcuts section.**

   The Dialing Shortcuts screen appears (see Figure 4-10).

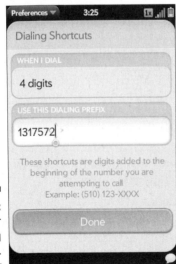

Figure 4-10:
Set your
dialing
shortcut.

4. **Tap the When I Dial section and select the number of digits you want to enter.**

   In this example, select four digits. (You can choose anywhere between four and seven digits.)

5. **In the Use This Dialing Prefix box, type the digits you want your Pre to add before it dials the number.**

   In this example, you type seven digits.

   The combination of prefix digits and digits you enter must add up to a complete phone number for the region you are calling (typically 7 or 11 within the United States, depending on whether you're dialing an area code).

6. **Tap Done.**

   Pre saves the dialing shortcut.

When you type a number into the phone dialing pad, the dialing shortcut kicks in after you dial the number of digits you supplied in Step 4. If you're not trying to dial someone in your company, just keep entering digits, and the Pre will ignore the dialing shortcut.

Using the keyboard to search for contacts in the phone dial pad

By default, when you display the phone dial pad but you use the Pre keyboard to enter a phone number, the only keys that actually operate on the keyboard are the number keys. But, if you'd like to be able to search for a contact by typing his name on the keyboard, you can set a preference that makes all keys on the keyboard active. When you then type on the keyboard, your Pre searches Contacts for the name you typed and supplies that contact's phone number so you can dial it.

To set the preference, follow these steps:

1. **On the Quick Launch toolbar, tap the Phone icon to launch the phone dial pad.**

2. **Tap the Sprint application menu at the top of the phone dialing pad, and on the menu that appears, tap Preferences.**

   The Phone Preferences screen appears; refer to Figure 4-9.

3. **In the When Typing in Dialpad section, tap the button beside Show Contact Matches so that it toggles from Off to On.**

If you display the phone dial pad and type using the Pre keyboard, your Pre will display phone numbers for contacts whose names match what you typed.

Receiving Calls

Initiating a call is one thing, but that's only half of the equation when it comes to a phone. You want to accept calls, too, right? Of course your Pre offers ways to manage incoming calls: to take the call or not. In addition, you can control the ringtone your phone sounds when calls come in.

Handling incoming calls

When a call comes in, you can answer it, or you can opt to ignore it. To answer a call, tap the green phone icon that appears in the lower-left portion of the screen (see Figure 4-11). To ignore a call, tap the red phone icon that appears in the lower right of the screen, also shown in Figure 4-11). When you ignore a call, the call rolls immediately to voice mail.

Figure 4-11:
When a call comes in, answer it or opt to ignore it.

Answer   Ignore

If you miss a call — say you turned off your phone and someone calls you — the Pre displays a message onscreen to alert you and also offers you the option to call back without checking first voice mail (see Figure 4-12). Tap Call Back or tap Dismiss, as appropriate.

Figure 4-12:
When you
miss a call,
choose
whether to
call back or
disregard.

Setting ringtones

You have choices for ringtones for your phone. You can select one of the
ringtone sounds that comes with the Pre, or you can download a song and
use the first few seconds of the song as the phone's ringtone.

The ringtone you select using the following steps applies to all incoming
phone calls. You can, however, set individualized ringtones for contacts; see
Chapter 8 for details.

To select a ringtone for your phone, follow these steps:

1. **Tap Launcher.**

2. **Swipe from right to left in Launcher until you find the Sounds and
   Ringtones app; tap that.**

   The Pre displays the main screen of the Sounds and Ringtones app
   (see Figure 4-13).

   Your current ringtone appears as the first item in the Ringer Switch On
   section.

3. **Tap that ringtone to see a list of possible ringtones (see Figure 4-14).**

4. **Tap the Play icon next to the name of the ringtone to preview it.**

Figure 4-13:
The Sounds
and
Ringtones
preferences
screen.

Preview a ringtone.

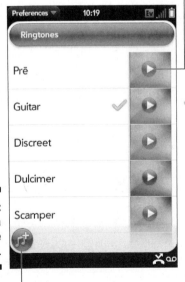

Figure 4-14:
Select a
ringtone
here.

Use a song for a ringtone.

5. **To set a particular ringtone as the one that sounds when your phone rings, tap and hold the ringtone.**

   When you release, the Pre sets the selected ringtone for your incoming calls.

6. **To select a song for your ringtone, tap the button in the lower-left corner of the screen shown in Figure 4-14.**

   Your Pre displays the available songs you've downloaded.

7. **To preview the song, tap to the right of the song title. To use the song as your ringtone, tap the song title.**

Set the ringtone volume by tapping, holding, and dragging the Ringtone Volume slider on the screen, as shown in Figure 4-13.

Silencing the ringer

You can silence the ringer on an incoming call and then answer it or let it ring through to voicemail. To silence the ringer, slide the Ringer switch at the top of the phone to the right into the Off position; you'll see a small red square on the top of the phone when the ringer switch is off. (Note that even with the ringer off, your phone will still vibrate when a call comes in.)

Silencing the ringer affects only the sound of incoming calls; you'll still be able to hear sounds from movies, videos, or music.

Ringtones, the law, and you

With the amount of press swirling around the RIAA (Recording Industry Association of America) and its pursuit of folk illegally downloading and distributing music, it's fair to ask whether turning a track you legally purchased (or otherwise acquired) into a ringtone is within the bounds of the law. The short answer is "yes." A recent court ruling determined that ringtones aren't considered derivative works of an artist, which would be subject to additional royalties. Some contention exists as to whether ringtones constitute a public performance of a song — another contingency that would demand that more money be paid to the publisher — but the Copyright Office's current stand is that they're for private use, even though others can hear them.

While You're on the Phone

While you're on the phone, you can take several actions. Using the Phone app (shown in Figure 4-15), you can do the following while a call is in progress:

 ✔ Tap the Speaker button in the lower left of the screen to place the call in Speaker Phone mode.

 ✔ Tap the Mute button (beside the Speaker button) to shut off the phone's microphone so that you can speak without being heard by the caller.

 ✔ Adjust call volume, using the Volume buttons on the left side of your phone.

Figure 4-15: Place a call in Speaker Phone mode or mute the microphone.

Speaker phone

Mute

You also can access the phone's dial pad by tapping the Keypad button (beside the Mute button), and you can add a call to your conversation; read on.

Working with a second call

While talking to one person, you can call another person. For example, you might be talking to John and need to check with Mary to see whether she's available for the meeting you and John are arranging. Tap the Add Call button in the lower right of the screen (refer to Figure 4-15). Your Pre places the first call on hold and presents you with the dial pad. Dial the second number, and Pre connects you to the second caller. Your phone screen will resemble the one shown in Figure 4-16.

One call on hold while you dial another

Figure 4-16: Fielding two calls at once.

If you're talking on the phone and another call comes in, you'll receive a "second call" notification. Tap the green phone icon beside the notification to answer the second call; Pre automatically places the first call on hold, as shown in Figure 4-17.

The appearance of the On Hold button changes, depending on whether you initiate both calls or one call was an incoming call. When you initiate both calls, the On Hold button looks like the one shown in Figure 4-16. When you initiate one call and then answer an incoming call, the On Hold button looks like the one shown in Figure 4-17.

Here are a couple things to keep in mind when using this feature:

✔ You can swap between calls only if the second call is an incoming call — not one that you initiate.

✔ To swap between calls, tap the On Hold button. Your Pre puts the active call on hold and switches to the other call.

✔ You can turn two separate calls into a three-way conference call *if* you have that service on your plan. ***Note:*** Minutes for both calls might be charged to your plan. To turn two separate calls into a three-way conference call, tap the On Hold button. The Pre connects all three calls.

One call on hold while you receive another

Figure 4-17: When you receive a call while talking, your Pre places the initial call on hold.

Saving a caller's number to Contacts

If you receive a call from a number that isn't in your Contacts, you can add that number to your Contacts either during or after the call. To add the number to Contacts during the call, tap the Add to Contacts button beside the caller's phone number (see Figure 4-18).

Pre displays a screen that offers you the option to save the number as a new contact, add it to an existing contact, or cancel the operation.

To add the number after you disconnect the call, tap the Call List button in the lower-right corner of the phone dial pad. A list of all calls made or received appears onscreen (see Figure 4-19). Find the number you want to add to Contacts and then tap the Add to Contacts button beside the phone number.

Add to Contacts

TIP

    ✔ **Green phone icons:** Calls you made

    ✔ **Blue phone icons:** Calls you received

    ✔ **Red phone icons:** Missed calls

You can sort the view to see only the calls you missed if you tap Missed Calls
at the top of the screen.

Pre opens the Contacts app and displays a new Contacts entry showing the
phone number. Tap the Add to Contacts button at the bottom of the screen
to choose whether to save the number as a new contact, add it to an existing
contact, or cancel the operation.

Switching to another app

While you're on a call, information about the call appears on the phone dial
pad. For example, if you call someone stored as a contact, the contact's name
appears above the dial pad, but you don't need to leave the phone dial pad
maximized onscreen. Suppose that you need to check your calendar while
you're on the phone. You can press the Center button to switch to Card View,
where you can open the Calendar from the Quick Launch toolbar or open
some other app using Launcher. While you're on a call and also working in
another app (like Calendar), you'll see a phone icon in the lower-left corner of
the screen (see Figure 4-20).

See all calls. See missed calls.

Figure 4-19:
Tap the Add
to Contacts
button
beside the
phone
number.

Call List button

Figure 4-20:
You see
a phone
indicator
(lower-left
corner) if
you're on
a call.

You're on a call.

Working with Voicemail

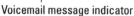

The commands in this chapter are specific to Sprint. Most will likely work on most other carriers, but just be aware.

When you get a voicemail message, you'll hear an alert sound. And, onscreen, you'll see an indicator that you have one or more voice mail messages waiting. The left screen of Figure 4-21 shows you the notification while working in the Phone dial pad, but you'll also see an indicator in the lower right of the Pre screen as you work in most other Pre apps on your phone, as shown in the right screen of the figure. For example, Figure 4-21 shows you the voicemail message indicator while working in Google Maps.

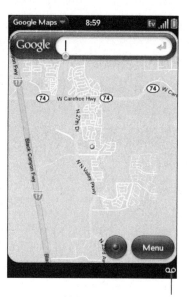

Figure 4-21: See how many voicemails you have.

Voicemail message indicator   Voicemail in another app

To check your voicemail messages, you can

- Tap the indicator that appears in the lower right of most screens. When you do, Pre displays another indicator that you can tap to dial voicemail.

- On the Phone dial pad, tap the Voice Mail button.

- My personal favorite: In Launcher, in Card View, or on the phone dial pad, use the keyboard to press and hold the number 1. Unless you're in the phone dial pad, you do need to use the Orange key for this shortcut. Also in the Phone dial pad, you can press and hold the dial pad's number 1.

Regardless of the method you use to retrieve voicemail, Pre displays the Phone dial pad and calls your voicemail.

The first time you access voicemail, you'll be prompted to set up a pass code and a greeting. Note that you can opt not to use a pass code.

When you call voicemail, if you opted to use a pass code, you'll be prompted to enter the code, followed by the pound (#) key. The voicemail auto-response tells you how many messages you have; and, if you have new messages, begins to play them, telling you the phone number from which each call came and the date and time of each message. See Table 4-1 for a list of keys you can press to manage and navigate messages while you are listening to voicemail.

Table 4-1	Voice Mail Action Keys
Key	**Action**
1	Replay the date, time, and phone number information for the message
3	Fast-forward eight seconds
4	Replay the message from the beginning
5	Rewind the messages a few seconds
6	Forward a message to another phone number
7	Erase
8	Return call
9	Save
0	All Options
#	Skip to next message

If you save messages, the next time you access voicemail, new messages will play before saved messages.

From the Voice Mail system's main menu, which becomes active after you listen to all messages, you can do the following:

✔ **Press 1** to listen to messages again.

✔ **Press 2** to send a message to another user.

✔ **Press 3** to change personal options such as your pass code, greeting, and whether you hear message identification information before each message plays.

✔ **Press 8** to place a call. When you place a call while working in voice mail, the voice mail system returns you to voice mail after you complete the call.

If you find that you continue to receive notifications of new voicemail messages after you listen to or delete all your messages, reset the voicemail count:

1. **Open the Phone dial pad.**

   To access the dial pad, tap the Phone icon on the Quick Launch toolbar at the bottom of the Pre main screen.

2. **Tap your carrier's name (most likely, Sprint) at the top of the screen to display the application menu.**

3. **Tap Preferences to display the Phone Preferences screen.**

4. **Drag down with your finger to scroll to the bottom of the list; then tap Voice Count Reset (see Figure 4-22).**

Figure 4-22:
Use Voice Count Reset to halt being notified of messages that no longer exist.

Text Messaging

You can use your Pre Messaging app to send and receive text messages or instant messages using an IM account you already have set up online. Using the Pre Synergy feature, the Messaging app gathers all your messages to and from the same contact or phone number into a single thread called a *conversation*, regardless of the type of messages you exchange. This technique helps you maintain your entire message history with a person regardless of the different accounts you happened to use to communicate. You can include up to 160 characters in a single text message.

Starting a text conversation

You use the Messaging app to send a message. Each time you send a message, you have the options of starting a new conversation or continuing an existing one. To start a new conversation, follow these steps:

1. **Tap the Launcher button.**

2. **Tap the Messaging app.**

   The Messaging screen lists people with whom you've exchanged messages. Below each person's name, you see the last thread of the conversation (see Figure 4-23).

   If you haven't used Messaging yet, you obviously won't see this list out of the gate.

Figure 4-23: The Messaging app displays the list of people with whom you've exchanged messages.

Tap to start a coversation.

3. **To start the new conversation, tap the icon at the bottom of the screen; see Figure 4-23.**

   A new empty screen appears (see Figure 4-24). In the upper portion of the screen, the messages you exchange will appear.

Figure 4-24:
When you start a new conversation, the upper portion of the screen is blank.

4. **At the top of the screen, enter a contact name or the phone number of the person to whom you want to send a message.**

   The Pre Universal Search feature searches through your contacts and displays phone number information for any matches.

5. **Type your message at the bottom of the screen.**

6. **Tap the icon beside your message to send it (see Figure 4-25).**

Figure 4-25:
Tap the icon beside your message to send it.

Tap to send message.

Continuing a text conversation

When you want to continue a conversation, follow these steps:

1. **Tap the Launcher button.**

2. **Tap the Messaging app.**

   The Messaging screen lists people with whom you've exchanged messages. Below each person's name, you see the last thread of the conversation (refer to Figure 4-23).

3. **To continue the conversation, tap the conversation.**

   Pre opens the conversation. In the upper portion of the screen, the messages you have already exchanged appear (see Figure 4-26).

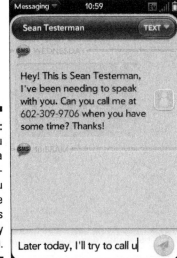

Figure 4-26: When you continue a conversation, you see the messages already exchanged.

4. **At the top of the screen, beside the contact's name, you can tap the Text button to select a phone number for the message.**

   If you have established an instant messaging (IM) account, you can select your IM account.

5. **Type your message at the bottom of the screen.**

   The Pre is smart enough to convert "u" to "you."

6. **Tap the icon beside your message to send it.**

Creating a multimedia message (MMS)

You can include pictures in your messages if your service plan includes multimedia messaging (also known as an MMS, or picture message). Follow these steps:

1. **In the Messaging app, start a conversation or continue an existing one. (See how in the preceding sections.)**

2. **Decide where to place the picture.**

   - *To add a picture to the top of the message:* Tap the paper clip icon in the lower-right portion of the screen before you start typing your message.

   - *To add the picture or sound file after you start typing:* Tap Messaging at the top of the screen. On the menu that appears, tap Add Picture.

   The Pre displays the screen you see in Figure 4-27.

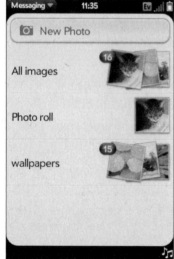

Figure 4-27: Use this screen to select a picture to include in your message.

3. **Tap one of the following:**

   - *New Photo:* This opens the Pre camera to take a photo to include in the message. After you take the photo, the Pre displays the photo with an Attach Photo button at the top; tap that button and the photo appears in your text message (see the left screen of Figure 4-28).

- *All Images:* This selects an existing picture to include in your message. Again, Pre displays the photo with an Attach Photo button at the top; tap that button, and the photo appears in your text message (see the right side of Figure 4-28).

Figure 4-28: Tap the Attach Photo button to include a photo in a text message.

You can send a text message while on the phone. Suppose that you're bragging about your kid's latest home run and want to send a photo of it. Minimize the phone app and open the Messaging app, create a message to the contact on the phone, and attach the photo.

Receiving text and multimedia messages

When you receive a new text message, your Pre displays a notification. Until you view the text message, you'll see a notification like the one shown in the lower right of Figure 4-29.

You can tap the notification to view open the Messaging app and view the message. If you've exchanged messages with the person who sent the message, Pre automatically adds the message to the existing conversation.

If the message includes pictures, videos, or music files, you can see, watch, or listen to them. In Figure 4-30, you see a photo sent by a friend in a text message.

Figure 4-29: The bubble in the lower-right corner indicates a text message.

Text message indicator

Figure 4-30: View pictures, watch videos, and listen to music included in text messages.

If you receive a text message that contains an image in JPG format (such as a photo) and you'd like to keep it on your phone, you can save the photo. Tap the photo in the text message, and Pre enlarges it and displays a Copy Photo button (see Figure 4-31). Tap it, and Pre saves the photo. You can then view the photo via the Photos app.

Figure 4-31:
Copy a
photo
received in
a text
message.

Save a photo from a text message.

To use the photo as your phone's wallpaper, connect your phone to your desktop computer, and tap USB Drive on the phone when prompted. Then, on your computer, copy or move the photo to the Wallpapers folder. When you disconnect the Pre from your computer, you can select the photo for your wallpaper using the Photos app.

If you receive a text message that contains a phone number, like the one shown earlier in Figure 4-26, you can dial that phone number by simply tapping it.

Managing text messages

You don't need to keep all your messages or conversations. To delete a message, slowly slide the message off the phone on the right side. The Pre displays a screen like the one shown in Figure 4-32. Tap Delete to delete the message.

To delete an entire conversation, open the Messaging app so that you display existing conversations. Slowly slide the conversation you want to delete off the right side. The Pre displays a screen like the one shown in Figure 4-32; tap Delete to delete the conversation.

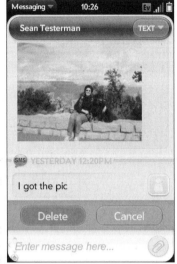

Figure 4-32:
Deleting
a text
message.

About instant messaging

You can use IM on your phone as long as you already have the account online. If you have an IM account with a provider that takes advantage of the Synergy feature, such as a GoogleTalk IM account, that IM account is automatically added to your phone when you enter your username and password for that provider in Email, Calendar, or Contacts. If you add an IM account later, follow these steps:

1. **Open the Messaging app.**

2. **Tap the Messaging application menu and choose Preferences & Accounts from the menu that appears.**

3. **Tap Add IM Account, select the account type, and provide your username and password.**

To sign into and out of your IM account while working in the Messaging app, use the Buddies tab that appears at top of the screen.

Tabs for Buddies and Conversations appear at the top of the Messaging app after you set up an IM account.

You send and receive IM messages the same way that you send and receive text messages; the only distinction becomes whether to start the message by tapping the Buddies tab for IM messages or the Conversations tab for text messages.

Chapter 5

Using Email

· ·

· ·

*O*f all the forms of communication that your Pre supports (and there are *many*), what's the most important? That's a very personal question, of course, and your answer could be totally different from the next Pre owner's — but there's at least a chance that you didn't say "calling people." In fact, recent studies have discovered that more ten percent of phone users today in some parts of the world don't even talk on their phone at all!

Even if calling people still ranks number one for you, though, odds are that you placed e-mail pretty high on your list. Virtually everyone has an e-mail account that they check on a daily basis now — some of us have several — and that makes it a particularly easy and convenient way to get in touch in a long-form way. It's quite often easier and less intrusive than calling someone, it's quicker than sending a letter via the regular mail, and it lets you send far more stuff than a text message. Long story short: E-mail isn't going anywhere. In fact, it's only going to get more important.

It should come as no surprise, then, that the Pre has excellent support for e-mail. It can handle multiple e-mail accounts at once; integrates seamlessly with the contacts stored on your phone; and allow you to send and receive a variety of popular attachment types, such as pictures, Microsoft Office documents, and Adobe Acrobat (PDF) files.

In this chapter, you'll see how to set up all your e-mail accounts on your Pre. You'll discover how to compose new e-mails, manage your inbox (and any other e-mail folders you may have), be notified when new e-mail arrives, attach photos and other files to your outgoing e-mails, and handle attachments as they come to you. In fact, by the time you're done mastering everything there is to know about e-mail on the Pre, you might not want to manage it from your PC anymore!

Setting Up Email

On the Pre, the application that you'll use to manage e-mail is simply called Email. Palm figures you'll be using this one pretty frequently, so an Email icon is placed on the Quick Launch toolbar by default, which means you can access it directly from Card View or Launcher by tapping the Email icon (the picture of the envelope) at the bottom of the screen. Just tap it to launch the application.

As discussed in Chapter 3, you can also get to the Quick Launch toolbar from wherever you happen to be on your Pre by dragging your finger up from the Gesture area, which causes the Quick Launch toolbar to appear. If you're getting to the Email icon this way, release your finger from the screen when it's directly below the Email icon — you'll know when your finger is in the right place because the icon will glow — and Email will launch.

If you customized your Pre and removed the Email icon from the Quick Launch toolbar (see Chapter 3 for details on how to do this), you'll instead find it in the Launcher.

Common e-mail services

Pre supports all the most common types of e-mail services found in the world today:

- **POP:** Post Office Protocol is a very simple way of accessing e-mail stored on a server. It's also very old and well established, which makes it the most commonly supported e-mail service type in the world. The main downside of POP is that it doesn't synchronize. For example, if you read an e-mail on your Pre, the e-mail server doesn't know that, so it doesn't let your PC or other devices that are connected to the same e-mail account know that you already read the e-mail. This makes managing your e-mail far more tedious if you use multiple computers.

- **IMAP:** Internet Message Access Protocol is a newer, more advanced standard than POP, but it's not supported by as many companies or Internet service providers (ISPs). Unlike POP, IMAP services keep track of what e-mails you've read and also do a better job of allowing you to organize your e-mail into multiple folders. IMAP is almost always preferred to POP, especially in situations where you're reading your e-mail on multiple computers.

- **Microsoft Exchange ActiveSync:** Also known as EAS, this service is a specialized type of e-mail account used internally by many companies that also includes integrated calendar and contact management. If you are using your Pre at a medium or large business, there's a good chance that you have an EAS account, but you might need to talk to your IT administrator before you're able to add it onto your Pre (especially if the Pre was not given to you by the company).

✓ **AOL, Hotmail, and other popular services:** The Email application knows details about the servers and protocols used by popular e-mail services, so you won't need to fill out very many details when setting these up.

Launching Email for the first time

The first time you launch Email, you'll be prompted to add an e-mail account (see Figure 5-1). Note that if you've set up an account through Contacts, Calendar, or Messaging — Google and Exchange ActiveSync accounts, in particular — the Pre might recognized that the account you added also has an e-mail account associated with it and automatically set it up for you. However, you can still add additional accounts using the following instructions.

Figure 5-1:
Adding a
new e-mail
account.

To start setting up your account

1. **On the Add an Account screen, enter your e-mail address and password in the fields provided.**

Even if your e-mail service has a username that is distinct from your actual e-mail address, the Pre needs only your e-mail address in the first field. If the application needs more information from you, it will collect it in the next screen.

2. Tap Sign In.

Based on your e-mail address, Email will attempt to determine the type of account to use. If it's a popular e-mail service like from Google, AOL, Yahoo!, or Hotmail, Pre knows how to set these up and will require no more information from you.

If you enter a less-common e-mail address, though, you'll be taken to another screen (as shown in Figure 5-2) where you'll be asked to enter details about the e-mail server that you're connecting to. Consult with the company or individual responsible running the e-mail account for these details.

Figure 5-2:
For some
e-mail
accounts,
Pre needs
more
informa-
tion before
you're all
set.

3. If more details are required to set up this account, fill them out and then tap Sign In again at the bottom of the screen.

Pre immediately starts synchronizing your new account so that e-mail is available on your phone. You will also be able to use this new account for sending e-mail. (See "Composing and Sending E-Mail," later in this chapter.)

Adding e-mail accounts

If you want to add additional e-mail accounts in the future, it's just as easy:

1. With Email open, tap the Email menu in the upper left of the screen.

2. **Choose the Preferences & Accounts menu item.**

   The Email application's Preferences & Accounts screen opens. (The Preferences & Accounts screen is discussed more in depth later in the chapter.)

3. **Scroll to the bottom of the screen and tap the Add an Account button.**

   You're taken through the same process as you when you first opened Email, starting by entering your e-mail address and password. (Refer to Figure 5-1.) When this is complete, your new e-mail account is added and automatically begins to synchronize.

Reading and Managing Your E-Mail All in One Place

After you configure your e-mail accounts, the first thing you'll see is a screen of inboxes and folders, as shown in Figure 5-3. Think of this view as your e-mail home base. From here, you can get a bird's-eye view of all your configured accounts, all their folders, and how many unread e-mails are in each.

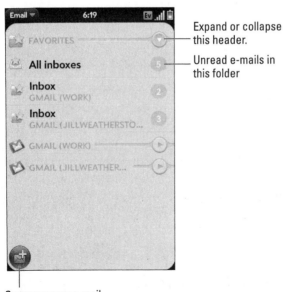

Expand or collapse this header.

Unread e-mails in this folder

Figure 5-3: Browsing the inboxes and folders in Email.

Compose new e-mail

One inbox to rule them all

Thanks to the hand-waving magic of Palm's Synergy technology (which I talk about in Chapter 1, and whose benefits you see throughout the book), Email automatically creates a single, unified inbox that contains incoming e-mail from all your accounts. That way, you don't need to bounce around from account to account to read everything sent to you. What's more, when you reply to e-mails within this view, Pre automatically knows what account was used to receive it and sends your reply using the same account.

This unified inbox is called All Inboxes, and it always appears at the top of the Favorites header. (You'll read more about favorites in the next section.) Tap the All Inboxes item to open it.

You see the contents of All Inboxes, as shown in Figure 5-4. All inboxes and folders that you use basically look like this when you open them — it's just a matter of which e-mails are shown to you in each account's inbox. Take a look at the All Inboxes features:

Inbox or folder name

Sender Name   Number of unread e-mails in this inbox or folder

E-mail preview   Subject   Time e-mail was received

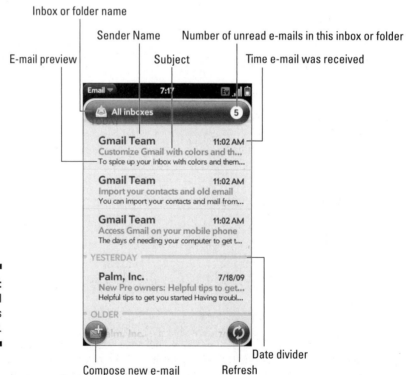

Figure 5-4:
The All
Inboxes
view.

Compose new e-mail   Refresh

Date divider

✔ **Inbox/folder name:** This shows you the name of the inbox or folder that you tapped to get there. If you were looking at the Sent Mail folder instead of All Inboxes, for example, the inbox name would read `Sent Mail`.

By tapping the inbox name in All Inboxes, you will be shown the names of each account whose e-mails are showing in the current view, the last time Pre updated itself with e-mails from that account, and the total number of e-mails shown.

✔ **Number of unread e-mails:** This is the number of unread e-mails that you can see in the current view, as shown in Figure 5-4. If you're looking at the inbox for a specific account rather than All Inboxes, this number will reflect only the number of unread e-mails in the current account.

✔ **Sender's name, subject, and time e-mail was received:** These are the standard fields that you're used to seeing in any e-mail account. When an e-mail is unread, these fields are bolded; after you read an e-mail, they will appear in a lighter font. If you're using an e-mail account based on IMAP (such as Google) or Exchange ActiveSync, e-mails will also appear as read here if they've been read somewhere else (on your desktop computer, for example).

✔ **E-mail preview:** A short, one-line preview of the beginning of the e-mail appears here.

✔ **Date divider:** Your e-mails are ordered chronologically, with the most recently received e-mails appearing at the top. To further help you distinguish what's new and what's stale, Email adds blue dividers above the e-mails received today, yesterday, and everything before that (labeled `Older`).

✔ **Compose New E-Mail:** The Compose New E-Mail button is available both at the top level of the Email application (when you're browsing all your inboxes and folders) and within e-mail views like All Inboxes. When you tap Compose New E-Mail, Email starts composing a new e-mail. You'll find out more about composing e-mails later in the chapter.

✔ **Refresh:** When you tap this button, Email immediately contacts your e-mail account and attempts to retrieve new e-mail. If you're in the All Inboxes view, all your accounts are contacted at once.

Individual accounts and favorites

Tap the arrow that appears on the right side of the blue line delineating each e-mail account to toggle between showing and hiding all the folders contained within it (see Figure 5-5). This list of folders is determined by the particular account and cannot be modified on your Pre. For example, with Gmail accounts, you'll automatically get a folder for each label that you created in your account.

Tap to collapse or open folder view.

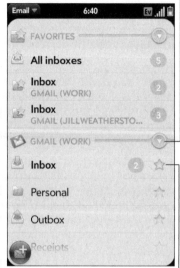

Figure 5-5:
An
individual
e-mail
account
expanded
to show
the folders
within it.

Favorite

At a minimum, you'll have

- ✔ An **Inbox,** where e-mails first arrive
- ✔ An **Outbox** for e-mails you've sent but have not yet transferred
- ✔ A **Trash folder** for deleted items
- ✔ A **Sent Mail folder** for e-mails that have successfully been sent
- ✔ And if you've saved any e-mails as drafts, a **Drafts folder** for e-mails that you're in the process of composing

Tap any folder to see the e-mails contained within them; the view will look basically the same as the All Inboxes view in Figure 5-4.

The names of the Trash, Drafts, and Sent Mail folders might vary depending on the type of e-mail account that you're using.

To the right of each folder in this list is a star, which indicates whether the folder is a *favorite*. Anything that you designate as a favorite appears under the special Favorites header positioned at the top of the screen (the same place where you find the All inboxes view) where it's easily accessible.

To make a folder a favorite, tap the star to the right of it. The star changes from gray to gold, and a duplicate of the folder appears under the Favorites header. To remove a folder from Favorites, tap the gold star to toggle it back to gray. Note that the folder will still be accessible; you'll just have to go look at the folders under the individual account where it's stored to find it.

To save space, the Favorites header can be collapsed the same way as individual accounts. Tap the down arrow on the right side of the blue line that denotes the Favorites section; the section collapses, and the arrow turns to face to the right. To expand it again, just tap the right-facing arrow.

Reading an e-mail

Regardless of whether you're in the All Inboxes view or a view for an individual account or folder, reading an e-mail is the same: Just tap it.

The e-mail appears onscreen (see Figure 5-6). While reading an e-mail, there are a number of things you can see and do:

- ✔ **Sender's name:** The name of the individual (or company) that sent you the e-mail.

- ✔ **Date and time e-mail was received:** Tapping either the sender's name or the date and time that the e-mail was received takes you to a full-screen list of details about the contact. If this contact is not already in the Contacts on your phone, an Add to Contacts button appears in the lower left of the screen that you can use to add the new e-mail address on the spot.

- ✔ **Recipient(s):** The names or e-mail addresses of the individuals who received this e-mail. This info is typically truncated if there are multiple recipients, but you can tap the field to expand it to see exactly how many people received it.

- ✔ **Subject:** The subject line of the e-mail.

- ✔ **Next older/next newer e-mail buttons:** Tap the arrows to the left and right of the subject line to quickly navigate to other e-mails in the view without having to go back (by swiping your finger to the left on the gesture bar) and choosing another e-mail from the list. If you want to read through all the e-mail in your inbox, this is a great shortcut.

- ✔ **Reply, Reply to All, and Forward:** These buttons work exactly as you'd expect them to in any e-mail program. You can find out more about sending e-mail later in the chapter.

- ✔ **Delete:** Tap this button to move this e-mail to the Trash folder.

Next newer e-mail   Date and time e-mail was received

Recipient(s)   Next older e-mail

Sender's name   Subject

Figure 5-6:
An
individual
e-mail.

Reply   Reply to All   Forward   Delete

Email can display plain text e-mails, but it can also display full HTML — the same stuff used on the Web — which means that you'll be able to see fancy formatted text and pictures just as you would if you were reading the e-mail on your PC using your Web browser or an e-mail client like Outlook or Entourage. (The e-mail shown in Figure 5-6 is an example of HTML e-mail.)

While reading an e-mail, a few features become available by tapping the Email menu in the upper left of the screen:

✔ **Mark as Unread:** When you open an e-mail on the Pre, it's automatically marked as read. If you want to return it to the unread state so that it appears bold in the list of e-mails, choose the Mark As Unread menu item.

For IMAP and Exchange ActiveSync accounts, this also causes the e-mail to appear unread on any other computers or devices that you use to access this account.

✔ **Set Flag:** This sets a flag on the e-mail that you can use however you like. Many people use this feature to indicate e-mails that they need to follow up on or reply to. After the flag is set, you'll see a picture of a flag on the right side of the subject line in the e-mail; and when you're looking at a list of e-mails — like in the All Inboxes view — flags appear on the left side of the screen. To clear a flag, return to the Email menu and tap the Clear Flag menu item.

Only one type of flag is available.

✔ **Move to Folder:** Choosing this menu item opens a new screen that displays all folders in your current e-mail account; tapping one of these folders moves the selected e-mail into that folder.

Handling attachments

It's not uncommon to receive pictures, documents, or other media attached to e-mails — and most of the time you won't have to wait until you get back to your PC to see or use them because the Pre does a commendable job of handling these attachments itself. Without installing any additional applications, the Pre can open the following file types:

✔ **Photo files:** JPEG, GIF, PNG, and BMP

✔ **Videos:** MPEG-4, H.263, and H.264

✔ **Music:** MP3, AAC, AAC+, AMR, QCELP, and WAV

✔ **Office documents:** Word, Excel, and PowerPoint

✔ **Adobe Acrobat PDF files**

When an e-mail arrives, you'll know that it has one or more attachments because of the paperclip icon between the sender's name and the time that the e-mail was received (see Figure 5-7).

Figure 5-7:
An e-mail in the Inbox with an attachment.

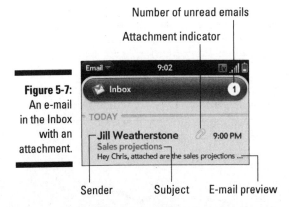

Number of unread emails

Attachment indicator

Sender   Subject   E-mail preview

After opening the e-mail, you'll find a new field right above the body that isn't typically there, which shows you how many files are attached to the e-mail and what their names are (see Figure 5-8). To open an attachment

1. **To expand it, tap the field above the e-mail body where the attachment file names are shown.**

   You see one line for each attachment of the e-mail. To the right side of each line, the attachment's file size is indicated.

   When e-mails are downloaded, attachments aren't automatically transferred (to save memory on your Pre). You can gauge the size of the attachment to help you decide whether you want to consume the memory necessary to transfer and open it.

2. **Press the attachment that you want to open.**

   The attachment line becomes a progress bar while the attachment is downloaded from the e-mail server. During this process, you can stop the download by tapping the X at the right side of the line.

   When the download is complete, the text of the attachment's file name changes from dim to bright.

3. **Tap the attachment again.**

   This second tap will either display the attachment within Email (in the case of photos, for example) or open the Pre application required to use this particular type of attachment.

When you open an attachment, you're only *viewing* it — you're not actually saving it to anywhere permanent in your Pre's memory, which means that if the e-mail that the file is attached to is deleted or is no longer accessible from your Pre, you will no longer be able to open it!

To save an attachment permanently on your Pre so that you can access it in the future, you can usually do so, but the way to do this will vary slightly depending upon the type of file:

- ✔ **For photos:** After tapping the photo in your e-mail to open it, tap the Copy to Photos button at the bottom of the screen. This copies the photo to your permanent collection of photos on the phone (accessible from the Photos application, which I cover in Chapter 11).

- ✔ **For most other file types:** When the application opens to view your file, tap the application menu in the upper left of the screen and then tap the Save As menu item. If you don't see this option, that means this particular type of attachment can't be permanently saved to your phone.

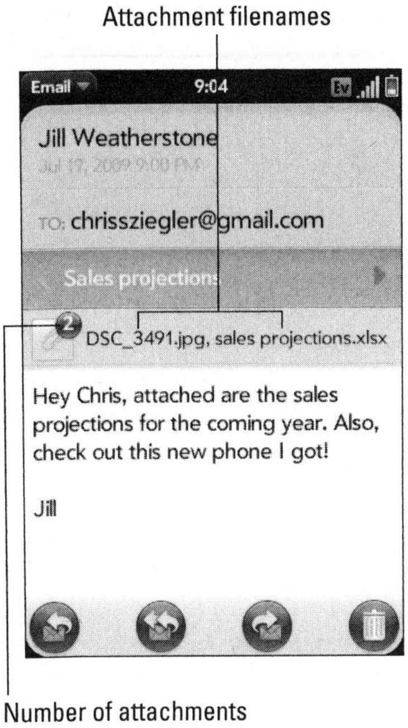

Attachment filenames

Figure 5-8:
Details
about
attachments
are shown
below the
e-mail
subject and
above the
body.

Number of attachments

Composing and Sending E-Mail

As I discuss earlier, Reply, Reply To All, and Forward buttons are available when you're looking at an e-mail — and that's one way to send an correspondence. You can also start a new e-mail from scratch by tapping the Compose button that appears at the bottom left of the folder view and every e-mail list in the application.

Regardless of what method you use to compose an e-mail, though, you start out with a screen that looks something like Figure 5-9 — the only difference is that if you already replied, replied to all, or forwarded, you'll have certain fields already filled out for you, just as you'd expect. The e-mail that you're forwarding or replying to will also automatically be added to the body of your new e-mail.

Tap to open Contacts.

Figure 5-9:
Composing
a new
e-mail.

Attachment button   Send

The parts of an e-mail

Take a look at the anatomy of a typical e-mail screen:

✔ **From:** This is the account used to send the e-mail. If you're composing a new e-mail from scratch, your default account will be used. (Read how to change the default account later in this chapter.) To change the account, tap this area of the screen and select the account you want to use from the list that appears.

✔ **To:** When you tap the To button on the left side of the screen, you can add CC (carbon copy) and BCC (blind carbon copy) fields to your e-mail, which work the same way as you'd expect in any e-mail application. Tapping the button a second time collapses the field so that only To is visible again.

To the right of the To button (and the CC and BCC labels when they're visible) is a text field where you can type an e-mail address or name of a contact that you want to send the e-mail to. As you type, Pre automatically searches your contacts and look for any matches; if it finds any, they are displayed below the text field, and you can tap them to select and add them.

Alternatively, tap the button with the Address Book icon that appears on the right side of the To field. This opens your entire Contacts list and allows you to scroll and select the e-mail address you want.

To send the e-mail to multiple recipients, separate each recipient with a comma. However, you don't have to use a comma if you're selecting recipients from your Contacts list — you can just keep selecting e-mail addresses, and the Email application will know how to handle them.

If you make a mistake and want to remove a recipient that you just added, press the Backspace key on the keyboard.

✔ **Subject line:** Type the subject of your e-mail here.

✔ **E-mail body:** This part is the Big Kahuna — the big, blank area where you do all of your typing.

The `Sent from My Palm Pre` signature that automatically appears in the body of the e-mail can be deleted by backspacing over it. Later in the chapter, you'll see how to set the Email application so it doesn't show up at all.

✔ **Attachment button:** In the lower left of the e-mail, tapping the Attachment button (shown as a paperclip) allows you to attach files. More on this in a moment.

✔ **Send button:** Press the Send button, and *voilà!* Your e-mail's off to the races. The Send button has a paper airplane on it, and you'll find it in the lower right of the e-mail.

When you compose an e-mail, it's placed in a new card. If you're not ready to send the e-mail right away, you can leave the card open and return to the main Email application card to read other e-mails (or to any other card, for that matter). If you close the new e-mail's card by flinging it off the screen, it's automatically saved to your drafts.

Attaching things to your e-mail

You're done addressing and writing your mail. Now you want to attach something. Just tap the Attachment button to bring up a new screen (attaching a photo is shown in Figure 5-10) where you choose the file to attach. The toolbar at the bottom of the screen bears four buttons, representing the four different kinds of files that the Pre allows you to attach:

✔ **Photos:** Any photo stored on your Pre will be shown here in the same organization that you see in the Photos application (which you can explore in Chapter 11). You can also take a new picture to attach by pressing the New Photo button at the top of the screen; you'll be taken to the camera viewfinder screen. (See Chapter 11 for details on how to use the camera.) After you snap the picture, you can attach it by tapping the Attach Photo button at the top of the screen.

✔ **Videos:** Although you can't use the Pre to record videos, any videos that you have stored on it can be attached and sent to your e-mail, and they will be shown here.

✔ **Audio:** Music, sound effects, and any other sound files that are stored on your Pre can be attached here.

Preview video and audio files before attaching them by tapping the Play button that appears at the right side of each item in the list.

✔ **Documents:** Miscellaneous documents — Microsoft Office and PDF files, for example — can be attached and will appear in this list.

After you tapped a file type to open its collection, tap an item there, select it, and attach it to your e-mail. *Note:* In the case of photos, the photo will be shown full-screen when you select it; then tap the Attach Photo button to complete the process. If you want to attach another file, repeat the process by tapping the Attachment button again.

Figure 5-10: Choose an attachment to send with this e-mail.

Photos   Audio

Videos   Documents

Setting Email Preferences

To configure settings for Email, you'll need to get into the Preferences & Accounts screen:

1. **Tap the Email menu in the upper left of the screen.**

2. **Choose the Preferences & Accounts menu item.**

From here, you'll find the following options available:

✔ **Smart Folders:** These are special folders that appear under your Favorites that Email automatically manages for you. The one that's turned on by default — All Inboxes — simply collects e-mail from all your accounts' inboxes into a single place. Similarly, All Flagged collects all e-mails that you flagged, regardless of the account that they're in. By default, All Inboxes is turned on, and All Flagged is turned off.

✔ **Accounts:** You'll see a line in this section for every e-mail account that you added to your Pre. You'll see some of the settings available within each account in detail next.

✔ **Default Account:** This is the account that the application uses by default for sending new e-mail. To change it, tap the account button below the Default Account header and then select the account you wish to use from the list that appears.

✔ **Add an Account:** Tap this button to add another e-mail account to the application. (See the section "Adding e-mail accounts," earlier in the chapter).

If you tap an individual account in the Accounts section of this screen, you're taken to another screen with specific settings for that account. The exact settings that you see here depend upon the specific type of account, but here are some of the interesting ones that you'll want to know about:

✔ **Account Name:** This is how the account is identified throughout Email (in the view of all folders, for example), so I recommend changing this to something descriptive and meaningful to you. For example, you could to rename your work e-mail account as "Work."

✔ **Full Name:** By changing this setting, you can change how you're identified on outgoing e-mails in the From field, and you can do this on a per-account basis.

✔ **Show Notification:** When this is set to On, you get a notification at the bottom of the Pre screen whenever you receive a new e-mail on this account.

✔ **Play Sound:** Setting this to On causes your phone to play a brief sound whenever you receive an e-mail on this account.

Sorry, but you can't choose the sound. You get what you get.

✔ **Vibrate:** If you want the Pre to vibrate when you get e-mail on this account, set this to On.

✔ **Signature:** As mentioned in "The parts of an e-mail" earlier in the chapter, the Pre appends a `Sent from My Palm Pre` signature to the end of every e-mail by default. If you wish to change this — or remove it altogether — you can do it by modifying this setting.

✔ **Reply-to Address:** When you send an e-mail and you want your recipients to reply to a different address than the one you're sending from, change this value.

✔ **Sync:** The Sync section has a couple settings that will affect how e-mail is displayed to you.

- *Show Email:* This setting determines how far back the Pre should go to get e-mail from your account; the default setting is 7 days, but you can choose values ranging from 1 day to All (if you want your Pre to retrieve every e-mail from your account, no matter how old it is).

- *Get Email:* This setting determines how often e-mail is retrieved. The default setting is 15 minutes. By setting this to As Items Arrive, your Pre will maintain a continuous connection to that account so that you receive new e-mail on your Pre the moment it is sent to you (this setting isn't available for all account types). On the opposite end of the spectrum, you can set it to Manual, which means that the Pre will never retrieve e-mail — you'll have to do it yourself using the Refresh button.

Battery life can decrease substantially when you set your Pre to check e-mail more frequently, so don't let it check e-mail more often than you think you need it to. You might want to spend several days playing with this setting and monitoring its effect on battery performance to determine how you want your Pre configured.

✔ **Default Folders:** To change the folders on your account that the Pre uses to store sent e-mail, drafts, and trash, use items in this group.

✔ **Remove Account:** Use this to remove an e-mail account from the Email application altogether.

✔ **Change Login Settings:** If you've changed your e-mail password, your Pre will no longer be able to connect to the account until you update your login settings. Use this setting to do that.

Chapter 6

Staying in Touch with Instant Messaging

*L*ong gone are the days when staying connected simply meant having a cellphone with you at all times that you could use to make and receive calls. Nowadays, you're probably inundated with text messages, multimedia messages, and everything in between. And it's not enough to just check your e-mail or your IMs when you come back to your computer, either — people expect you to be on top of *that*, too — and reply. How the heck are you supposed to manage all this from a phone?

For starters, Pre supports the most popular IM services, which makes it easy to stay connected to AOL Instant Messenger (AIM), Google Talk, and others when you're away from your desk. And to help you keep your sanity while you get blasted with all those IMs, Synergy technology from Palm saves the day by helping you keep everything organized in one place. You don't need to hop between several different accounts, programs, and devices to see everything being said to you.

In principle, text messages, multimedia messages, and IMs are quite similar: With all these technologies, the idea is that you're exchanging very short messages with others in real time. The Pre OS — webOS — capitalizes on that similarity by grouping all these types of messages into a single place, ordered chronologically into a *thread*. Whether you're sending a text message through your network provider (Sprint, for instance) or an IM through Google Talk, they all show up on the same screen on your Pre in the order that you sent them.

Of course, Synergy doesn't help you receive fewer messages. (You'll have to start telling some of your friends and family members to get lost if you want to accomplish that.) However, by grouping messages, managing the messages you *do* receive is much more manageable.

In this chapter, you'll find out everything you need to set up your favorite IM accounts on your Pre so that you're never more than a couple swipes of a finger away from chatting with your buddies. You'll also see how to respond to incoming messages, see who's online, change your status (in other words, alert people that you're "away," whether you really are or not), and manage notifications when someone messages you.

Getting Started with Messaging

Because Pre uses Synergy to group several forms of messaging into a single application, there isn't a dedicated app for instant messaging. Instead, IM gets bundled into the unified Messaging application along with text and multimedia messaging (covered in Chapter 4).

To launch Messaging, open Launcher and tap the Messaging icon. As you'll discover in the "Instant Message Notifications" section later in the chapter, incoming messages can cause notifications to appear on your Pre, too, which you can in turn use to open Messaging. In other words, you won't necessarily always need to go all the way into Launcher to open Messaging, and this shortcut is especially convenient for those serial messengers out there who can't go more than a minute or two without responding!

Creating an IM account

Lots of folks have multiple IM accounts that they use regularly, and the Pre can handle them all with aplomb. Pre works so seamlessly, in fact, that you won't even know what service you're using to talk to people in your buddy list (unless you want to!).

The first time you open Messaging, you're prompted to add an IM account (see Figure 6-1). If you've already added certain types of accounts to the Calendar, Contacts, or Email applications that also feature IM capability (Google, for example), you see those automatically listed here for you.

Figure 6-1:
You're
prompted
to add an
account the
first time
you open
Messaging.

Because Messaging is also used for text and multimedia messaging, your phone number is listed on this screen as a type of account under a separate Text Messaging section.

If you don't want to add any additional accounts to Messaging at this time, that's fine: Just tap the Done button and continue using the application. On the other hand, if you want to create an IM account now, here's the path:

1. **Tap the Add an Account button.**

2. **Tap the button of the type of account you want to add.**

   At the time of this writing, Google Talk and AOL Instant Messenger (AIM) were available, but more might become available by Palm.

3. **In the screen that opens, enter your username and password for the account that you select (see Figure 6-2).**

4. **Tap the Sign In button.**

   You are returned to the Add an Account screen, and the account that you just added now appears in your list of accounts.

   If you have more than one IM account that you want to add, you can keep repeating Steps 1–4 until they've all been added.

5. **When you're finished, tap Done.**

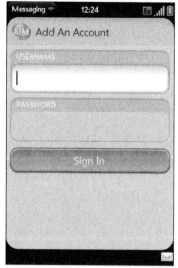

Figure 6-2:
Adding a
new AIM
account.

Adding additional IM accounts

You can add new IM accounts at any point in the future. To do so, follow these steps:

1. **Launch Messaging.**

2. **From the Conversations/Buddies screen, tap the Messaging menu in the upper left of the screen.**

3. **Tap the Preferences & Accounts menu item.**

   The Preferences & Accounts screen appears, which you can read about in depth later in the chapter.

4. **Tap Add IM Account.**

5. **Tap the button corresponding to the type of IM account you want to add.**

6. **Enter your username and password for the account that you select.**

7. **Tap the Sign In button.**

   The account is added, and you are returned to the Preferences & Accounts screen. Toward the bottom of this screen, in the Accounts section, you'll see that your new account has been added.

Seeing Your Buddy List

After you finish setting up your IM accounts for the first time, you're taken to the Buddies screen, as shown in Figure 6-3. This is what many IM programs call a *buddy list*, and it's simply a list of all your IM contacts and their *status* (whether they're available). Take a look at some of the features of the buddy list:

Name

Buddy status   Buddy icon

Figure 6-3:
The Buddies
screen.

New Message

Custom message

✔ **Buddy status:** This color-coded dot indicates whether your buddy is available to take instant messages.

- *Green:* That buddy is available.

- *Orange:* That buddy is busy or away.

- *Gray:* That buddy is offline.

By default, you won't see buddies who're not online. After all, if you have a lot of buddies, seeing that many names would clog your buddy list and make it difficult to use. If you want to see them all, though, you can enable them by tapping the Messaging menu and choosing the Show Offline Buddies menu item. Conversely, if offline buddies are showing and you want to make them go away, tap the Messaging menu and choose Hide Offline Buddies. This feature also allows you to see all your buddies' screen names even when you're not signed in.

✔ **Name:** This is the buddy's username (or *screen name,* as it's sometimes called). If you have this screen name saved as a contact on your Pre, the phone will automatically figure out the association and show the person's real name (from Contacts) rather than the screen name.

✔ **Custom message:** Some types of IM accounts allow users to add a special message displayed next to their screen name in other users' buddy lists. If a contact has a custom message set up, you'll see it here.

✔ **Buddy icon:** The picture that your buddy has self-assigned displays here. If you don't have a picture for this buddy in Contacts, Pre automatically adds the buddy icon (that your buddy assigned himself) to your Contacts list.

✔ **New Message:** Tapping this button starts a new message, which I cover later in the chapter.

The buddies that you see in this list are loaded from your IM accounts, meaning that if you remove a buddy from your AIM account on your PC, for example, it'll disappear from your Pre as well. Likewise, if you add a new buddy on your PC, it'll appear on your Pre the next time you log in.

Because Synergy technology is in use here, you won't merely see separate buddy lists for every account you added: You see a single, unified buddy list that spans all your IM accounts (some popular IM programs for PCs like Trillian, Pidgin, and Adium work the same way). If a buddy has more than one account and you have her added to the same contact in your Contacts, she will be grouped together in the buddy list. *Note:* You can still choose what type of IM service to use to talk to the buddy after you start a conversation. I discuss this later in this chapter.

Managing Your Status

When you use your IM accounts on your PC, setting your status allows you to indicate to your IM contacts whether you're available to chat. Some common statuses are Available and Busy although these descriptors might vary depending upon the type of IM software you're using.

Just like the IM software you use on your PC, Pre allows you to set your status to Busy. That way, you can stay signed into your IM accounts but not feel obligated to immediately respond. (Of course, the phone is really just sitting there in your pocket waiting to be used even though your status is set to Busy, but that's our little secret, isn't it?)

Are you available?

Similar to some computer-based IM programs like iChat, the Pre also uses status to determine whether you're signed into your accounts. In all, three statuses are available:

- ✔ **Available:** To your IM contacts, it appears as though you are available to chat. You will likely get more IMs this way, so be prepared to get messages early and often.

- ✔ **Busy:** Think of the Busy status as a catch-all when you don't want to be bugged. Pre doesn't have an Away status, per se, so Busy is the best choice when you need to let your IM contacts know that you can't respond to their messages right now.

- ✔ **Sign Off:** When you choose Sign Off, you sign off all IM accounts that you have configured in Messaging. That means that you can't IM others, you can't see who is online, and others can't IM you or see you online. There is one exception to this rule: Some services — Google Talk, for example — allow your IM contacts to message you even when you're offline, and the message will be delivered the next time you sign in.

To set your status, follow these steps:

1. **Tap the circle immediately above your buddy list on the left side of the screen.**

   A list of available statuses appears (see Figure 6-4).

2. **Tap the item in the list corresponding to the status you want to set.**

Whenever you change status, the dot in the center of the circle that you tap changes color to indicate your current status:

- ✔ **Green:** You are available.

- ✔ **Orange:** You are busy or away and are unable to answer IMs.

- ✔ **Gray:** You are not signed in.

Figure 6-4:
Choose
the status
shown to
your IM
contacts in
their buddy
lists.

When you're not signed in and you choose a status of Available or Busy, you immediately become signed in (assuming that you currently have a Wi-Fi connection or cellular reception). You are always signed in or signed out of all IM accounts at the same time; there is no way from this screen to only sign into certain IM accounts and leave other ones signed out, for example.

Custom messages

Earlier in this chapter, I mention the possibility of seeing a buddy's custom message right in your buddy list. (Refer to Figure 6-3.) Basically, this short message (if used) always displays with the buddy's name and status. For instance, if a buddy sets her status as Busy but she's really there, she might set her custom message to be I'm here, but please contact me only if it's an emergency. You can use your custom message for whatever you like, of course, but it's quite often used to give more information about the status that you've set.

You can control your custom message right from your Pre, and what's more, it'll automatically set that custom message on all your IM accounts at once — you don't need to go in and set it for each account individually. To do this, follow these steps:

1. **Tap the area immediately to the right of the circle that you use to set your buddy status.**

This area contains your current custom message. By default, it's the same as your status. So, when your status is Available, the custom message will simply read `Available`.

2. **Type your custom message (see Figure 6-5).**

3. **When you finish typing the message, tap the check mark at the right side of the screen.**

   Your custom message is set and will remain until you change it.

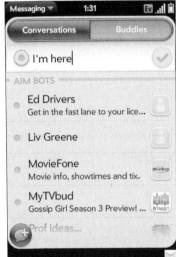

Figure 6-5:
Setting your
custom
message.

Striking Up a Conversation

With your buddy list under your belt, it's time to talk to someone. After all, that's what IM is all about, right?

To get started, just tap a buddy's name in your buddy list. A new conversation screen appears (see Figure 6-6), which is where the conversation with your buddy will take place. And because this is a *unified* conversation, it doesn't matter whether you're talking with your buddy by text message or IM: The entire conversation appears here, displaying in chronological order. You can seamlessly move from text message to AIM to Google Talk with your friend, and it'll all look like a single conversation to you. In Figure 6-6, for example, notice that I hopped from AIM to Google Talk.

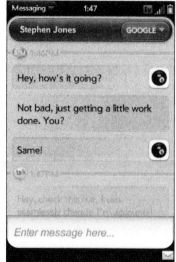

Figure 6-6:
You can hop
between
different IM
accounts.

Choosing a service to use for the conversation

When the conversation screen is open, you'll see the name or IM screen name of the buddy you are chatting with in the gray bar in the upper left of the screen. (This helps you avoid getting your buddies confused.) On the upper right of that gray bar, you see which type of messaging service will be used for the next message that you send. To you, it makes very little difference what messaging service you use to send the message because the Pre combines all the services into a single conversation — but at times, you may want to switch services on the fly; for example, if the buddy with whom you're chatting is in front of an office PC that only has access to certain services, you might want to switch to that service to make sure your messages are getting through to your buddy intact. To change the service

1. **Tap the button on the right side of the gray bar at the top of the conversation screen.**

   A menu of available messaging services appears. Depending on what information you entered for this buddy in your Contacts, you might see several different categories and accounts, including Text, AIM, and Google Talk.

2. **Tap the item of the service that you want to use.**

Every time you change IM services, a line appears across the conversation screen with the service's icon and a timestamp at the left. This line indicates that all messages appearing after that line were sent (and received) using that service.

Go on — say something

To talk to a buddy, tap the white area at the bottom of the conversation screen that reads `Enter message here`. Then start typing. When you finish, either tap the Send button (the paper airplane on the right side of the new message) or tap the Enter key on the keyboard. Your message is sent right away.

Managing conversations

Because you might be carrying on a number of conversations with different people at the same time, Pre allows you to have as many conversations going at once as you need. But how do you manage all of those?

First, return to your buddy list from the conversation screen by swiping your finger to the left on the gesture bar. (As discussed in Chapter 3, this is a *back gesture*.) At the very top of the Buddies screen is a bar with two buttons; Buddies selected by default. The other button is Conversations. Tap the Conversations button to see a list of all "live" conversations (you're currently engaged in; see Figure 6-7). The list is presented chronologically so that the most recently active conversations (meaning the last time you sent or received a message) are at the top.

From the Conversations screen, you can see the last thing written in each conversation (the text below the buddy's screen name) and who wrote it (the arrow to the left of it indicates who). If the arrow points to the right, you received this message; if the arrow points to the left, you sent it.

From here, you can tap any item in the list to return to the screen for that conversation. You can also delete entire conversations if you don't want to see them anymore:

1. **Place your finger on the conversation in the list that you want to delete and swipe either left to right or right to left.**

   The conversation is replaced by a gray bar with two buttons: Delete and Cancel (see Figure 6-8).

2. To delete the conversation, tap Delete. Otherwise, tap Cancel.

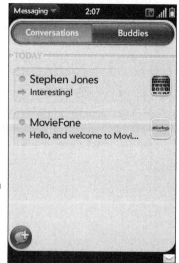

Figure 6-7:
The Conver-
sations
screen.

Figure 6-8:
Deleting a
conversa-
tion from
the Conver-
sations
screen.

Instant Message Notifications

After you sign into your IM accounts, you don't want to sit around in the Messaging application and wait for someone to message you. Heck, you probably don't even want to sit there with your phone in your hand — you want to put it back in your pocket, your holster, your purse, or wherever you keep your Pre, just as you normally would. So how do you know when someone tries to reach you via IM?

The answer lies in notifications. Like many webOS applications, Messaging supports notifications to let you know when important things happen (like receiving a new message). Whenever you're signed in and someone messages you, you receive a notification at the bottom of the screen with a preview of the message that was sent (see Figure 6-9). After a moment, this message disappears and is replaced by a small bubble icon in the lower right of the screen to remind you that you have unread IMs awaiting you. Tapping this icon takes you straight into the conversation so that you can immediately read the full message and reply.

Figure 6-9:
You have a
new IM!

Stephen Jones: Hey, are you there?

If you don't want to be notified when you receive IMs, no problem. Just turn them off. You'll find out how to do that in the next section.

Setting Preferences

To change the preferences and settings that the Messaging application uses, you must be in either the Conversations screen or the Buddies screen:

1. **Launch Messaging and navigate to either the Conversations screen or the Buddies screen.**

2. **Tap the Messaging menu in the upper left of the screen.**

3. Tap the Preferences & Accounts menu item.

The Preferences & Accounts screen appears.

Here are the items available in this screen:

- ✔ **Show Notifications:** If you want to receive a notification whenever you're signed in to your IM accounts and you receive a new message from a buddy (as discussed in the preceding section), set this to On; if you don't, set it to Off.

- ✔ **Play Sounds:** In addition to a visual notification, a sound can be played whenever you receive a new message. To play a sound, set this to On.

- ✔ **Accounts section:** Here is where you can see all the IM accounts configured for use in Messaging. You will also see your phone number listed in this section for text and multimedia messaging, but you can't reconfigure or remove this. If you change the password for any of your accounts or you wish to remove an account, tap its item in the list here and follow the onscreen prompts.

- ✔ **Add IM Account:** Tap this to add a new IM account, as I discuss earlier in the chapter.

Part III
Organizing Your Life

The 5th Wave   By Rich Tennant

"Well, here's what happened—I forgot to put it on my 'To Do' list."

In this part . . .

*P*alm has always been known for making powerful, full-featured, easy-to-use organizers, even before the days when its devices were cellphones, too. (This was back before the last Ice Age, if you recall.) The Pre continues that important tradition with a full suite of tools that will keep your schedule on track and your contacts just a couple taps of the finger away.

You'll discover the Pre's contact management in Chapter 8 and the Calendar functions in Chapter 9, but you'll also find out about a cool new feature that takes organization to a whole new level in Chapter 7: Universal Search. With Universal Search, nearly all of the most important information that's stored on your Pre can be searched from one easy place. Think of it as an industrious researcher built into your phone, ready to serve you 24/7 (and don't worry, he doesn't need any food, sleep, or vacation time).

Chapter 7

Searching for Anything and Everything

*T*he Pre and webOS seek to help you tackle a truly epic task: organizing every aspect of your life into one convenient place. Oh, and it just so happens that that "convenient place" just happens to be small enough to fit into your pocket! That's no small feat, requiring ease of use, a lot of really unique functionality, a wide variety of great applications — and a way to sort and find it all.

On the Pre, digging through all your information to find the golden nugget you're looking for is a two-pronged approach. Your main line of offense is something *Universal Search,* which (as you might have guessed) tries to wrap all your searching needs into a single place. Sometimes, though, you need more searching power than Universal Search can provide; for those times, you work with individual applications to drill down to your data.

Searching on the Pre isn't just about *your* data, though; it's also about the world's data! Palm knows that "Googling" has become an ingrained part of our vernacular, and that we spend as much time (if not more) looking stuff up on the Internet as we do looking up our own contacts. Consequently, Palm has integrated some really fantastic Internet searching capability.

In this chapter, you'll see how to find everything you need on the Pre (and maybe a few things you don't). You'll discover how easy it can be to get the information you're looking for, whether it's a colleague's phone number, an application, a song, or Macaulay Culkin's birthday (August 26, by the way).

Performing a Universal Search

Although Palm refers to this search capability as *Universal Search,* that's not quite accurate. Instead, think of it more as "a search for 80 percent of the stuff I'm looking for." That's still a pretty good percentage, though, and later in the chapter, you'll discover how to find everything else you need.

So, what exactly can you find (or do) with Universal Search? A few things:

- ✔ **Contacts:** Search through all contacts linked to your Palm Profile, regardless of where they come from (Google, Facebook, Exchange, and so on).

- ✔ **Applications:** After you install a bunch of applications from the App Catalog, quickly launching them can be tricky when you have to find just that one icon in Launcher. Universal Search helps you find the right app that you're looking to launch.

- ✔ **Google:** Ah, Google. Where would we be without you? Universal Search lets you run a Google Web search with a single press of a button.

- ✔ **Google Maps:** Instead of running a regular Google Web search, you can also invoke Google Maps if you're searching for an address or a location by name.

- ✔ **Wikipedia:** Although not always spot-on accurate, Wikipedia is by far the most comprehensive encyclopedia on the Web — and the Pre puts you just a press of a button away from it.

- ✔ **Twitter:** Think of Twitter as a huge roundtable discussion with a bunch of private and semi-private discussions going on 24/7 — that makes it a great place to see what the world is talking about in real time. The Pre lets you mine Twitter to find out what the hot topics are. (Even if you don't find it useful, it's endlessly entertaining!)

- ✔ **Placing a phone call:** You can also directly dial a phone number from the Universal Search screen, which saves you from having to go all the way into the Phone application.

To begin a Universal Search, you need to be either in Card View or in Launcher. (Read about both in Chapter 3.) From either place, just start typing on the keyboard. Pre will know what you're trying to do and immediately open the Universal Search screen.

Searching Contacts

If you were thinking of opening the Contacts application just to find someone by name, think again. You can do everything you need right from the comfort and convenience of Card View:

1. **From Card View or Launcher, start typing a part of the person's name whose information you want to find.**

   The Universal Search screen appears, and the letters you type appear at the top of the screen.

   You can search by first name, last name, or both. If you type just a first name, though, odds are good that you'll have more search results to sift through. (After all, how many Johns do you know?)

   While you type, contacts appear below your text. See Figure 7-1, where I searched for "jones."

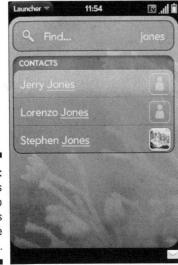

Figure 7-1:
Contacts start to appear as you type your search.

2. **When you see the contact you're looking for, tap it to call up that person's information.**

Alternatively, you can keep typing until only a single contact matches your entry. When this happens, Pre recognizes that this can be the only contact you're looking for and automatically shows all that contact's information (as shown in Figure 7-2).

Figure 7-2:
A contact's info appears when no other contact can match what you type.

With just a single contact's information showing in Universal Search, tapping different pieces of information triggers different actions, just like they do in the Contacts application (which I cover in depth in Chapter 8). For example, you can tap

- ✔ **A phone number:** The selected number is immediately dialed.

- ✔ **The SMS button:** In Figure 7-2, note the small button labeled SMS to the right side of each phone number. Tap this to start composing a new text message to that phone number instead of dialing it.

  Read all about SMS in Chapter 4.

- ✔ **An e-mail address:** The Email application opens, and you're immediately taken to a new e-mail with the selected e-mail address already filled out for you.

- ✔ **An IM address:** The Messaging application opens where you can begin composing a new instant message (IM) to the selected address. The Pre knows what kind of IM address this is (AOL, Google, and so on) from the information you entered about the contact, and automatically uses the correct account to make the connection. In other words, if you select an AOL IM address, your Pre knows to being composing a new IM message using your AOL account.

If a contact has a phone number assigned, pressing the Enter key on the keyboard immediately dials the first phone number assigned to that contact. Press Enter after that contact's information is displayed in Universal Search.

Searching for an application

When you first got your Pre, there weren't too many applications installed out of the box — fewer than three dozen, if you include all the settings screens — so it might not have been worth your time to type an application by name to find it and launch it. After a while, though, you'll probably find yourself installing dozens of additional applications through the App Catalog, and with each new installation, it'll get just a little harder to quickly find what you're looking for by scrolling through your Launcher.

Searching *for* an application is different than searching *within* an application. I cover that later in the upcoming section, "Searching in Applications."

And that's where Universal Search comes into play:

1. **Start typing the name of an application that you're looking for from Card View or Launcher.**

   Matching applications immediately start to appear as icons, as shown in Figure 7-3. Notice in the example here that the contacts matching "Sprint" appear in a list below the matching application icons. If you wanted to see one of those contacts' details instead of launching an application, tap the contact you want, and its details would open, just like what I describe in the preceding section.

Figure 7-3:
Search for
applications.

2. **Tap the icon of the application you want to open.**

   Universal Search hides, and the selected application immediately starts in a new card.

Searching Google

How many Web searches would you say you conduct on Google each and every day? 3? 5? 10? 50? For many, Google is the home base of the Internet and the first stepping stone to get to the information and Web sites that you need. Happily, with Universal Search, Pre makes Google just as easy to search as your own contacts:

1. **From Card View or Launcher, start typing the term (or terms) that you want to search for on Google.**

   If the term that you're searching appears in any of your contacts or applications, Pre assumes that you're looking for those and will not show you Internet search options by default.

   For example, if you type **Sprint**, you might have both applications and contacts with the word "Sprint" in them — so the Pre shows you those, but does not show you any Internet search options. In this case, the Pre has incorrectly guessed that you're looking for something in your phone's memory rather than for something on the Internet. It's an easy problem to fix, though, as you'll see in Step 2.

2. **If applications or contacts are showing, tap the Find bar at the top of the Universal Search bar.**

   In this example, you see four buttons directly below the Find bar: Google, Google Maps, Wikipedia, and Twitter (see Figure 7-4). Note the application and Contacts search results directly below those.

3. **Tap the Google button.**

   The Web application opens in a new card, and Google search results for your entered search term will appear. Figure 7-5 shows the result.

At this point, you can press links in the Web application and carry on with your Googling ways.

The Find bar

Internet search options

Searching Google Maps

The Google Maps capability built into the Universal Search is one of those, "Oh, wow!" moments. You'll be shocked and amazed by how useful this is (and by how frequently you end up using it).

Have you ever been walking or driving around and suddenly had an urge for pizza? Or maybe a good Chinese place, a dry cleaner, or a walk-in clinic? Many modern smartphones like the iPhone already make it pretty easy to find this information on a map, but with Universal Search, it's even easier because you don't need to go into a mapping application first — you just start typing.

Say you're looking for a pizzeria near you:

1. **From Card View or Launcher, type** pizza **(as shown on the left side of Figure 7-6).**

Search for location.

Figure 7-6: Search for pizza using Universal Search.

Tap to go to map.

2. **Tap the Google Maps button.**

If you have any applications or contacts with the word "pizza" in them, you first have to tap the Find bar before the Google Maps button will be visible.

As soon as you tap the Google Maps button, the Google Maps application appears in a new card, and shows you at a glance all the places where you can satiate your hunger for some Italian pie. See the result on the right side of Figure 7-6.

Here's where the magic happens: Google Maps automatically locates your position within a few hundred feet, which allows it to find pizza that's actually near you — you don't need to tell the application where you are! Read about Google Maps in detail in Chapter 12, but feel free to play around with it in the meantime — I can't blame you if you're hungry.

For Google Maps to be able to determine your location, you have to agree to the Google Mobile Terms of Service when you first set up your Pre, which I discuss in Chapter 2. If you didn't do that and you've changed your mind, you can do it at any time by tapping the Location Services icon in Launcher.

Searching Wikipedia

Wikipedia dubs itself as The Free Encyclopedia, and that's exactly what it is. Because anyone can contribute to it (even you!), it's extremely comprehensive, and you can find an article about just about any subject you can fathom. However, the freedom of anyone posting info is a double-edged sword because that also means the information you find hasn't necessarily been vetted for accuracy. Use and enjoy Wikipedia liberally, but use it at your own risk!

To kick off a Wikipedia search

1. **From Card View or Launcher, start typing the subject you'd like to learn more about.**

2. **Tap the Wikipedia button, below the Find bar.**

Like with the other types of Internet searches, you need to tap the Find bar to get the Wikipedia button to display if you have any contacts or applications on your Pre that contain the search term that you enter.

The Web application opens in a new card, and Wikipedia is loaded. If an article exists for the term you entered, it's shown (as in Figure 7-7); if not, you'll be informed that no article was found.

Figure 7-7:
Search
Wikipedia
on the fly.

Searching Twitter

Twitter is nothing more than a continuous stream of people around the world writing very short messages (140 characters maximum) to one another. That might not sound like something you'd want to search, but Twitter is so popular that it's actually a really good indication of hot topics — things that the world are talking about right this second.

For example, say you want to know what the world thinks about Brad Pitt right now (because, let's be honest, everyone has an opinion on the guy). It's easy:

1. **From Card View or Launcher, type** brad pitt.

2. **Tap the Twitter button, below the Find bar.**

   As usual, you have to first tap the Find bar to get the Internet search options to appear if you have any contacts or applications that contain the phrase "brad pitt." (And if you have Brad Pitt's contact information in your Pre, odds are you don't need to search for information on the guy — you can just call him up yourself.)

   The Web application opens in a new card, and you're taken to Twitter's search results page for your search term — in this case, "brad pitt" (see Figure 7-8) — where you can see everything that's recently been said about the guy. Looks like people like him quite a bit — what else is new?

Figure 7-8:
Twitter
search
results.

Placing a Call to a Contact You Found with Universal Search

The Pre was built from the ground up to save you time and effort as you go about common, everyday tasks. And as phones go, it really doesn't get any more common than dialing a phone number. This doesn't really qualify as a search, per se, but Universal Search has a shortcut that allows you to dial a phone number directly from Card View or Launcher without having to go into the Phone application first, which saves you a couple of valuable finger presses:

1. **With Card View or Launcher showing, dial the number you wish to call, using the orange numeric keys on the keyboard.**

   As long as you don't press any non-numeric keys, your Pre recognizes that you might be trying to enter a phone number as you do this — you don't need to hold down the Orange key to indicate that you're entering numbers.

2. **When you finish entering the number, press the Enter key on the keyboard or tap the number onscreen.**

   The number is immediately dialed.

When you finish entering the phone number, Universal Search gives you the option of creating a new contact using that number with a new button that appears directly below the number. Just tap it, and the contact is created; you'll be able to enter other pertinent details before saving it. That way, you won't have to enter the number next time — you'll be able to search for it by name.

Searching in Applications

To this point, I have shown you how to use Universal Search to find most of the stuff you'll need on a daily basis — contact information, applications, locations, and several different kinds of information on the Web. Of course, that leaves a lot of other stuff that could be searched.

Much of that "other stuff" is buried in individual applications installed on your Pre. There's no universal, catch-all rule for searching these applications — and obviously, I can't know what applications you specifically have installed — but there *is* a rule: If you see a list of anything, just start typing.

Take a common example: music. Say you're looking for a specific song; one option would be to select the Songs item on the Music Library screen, and scroll through the alphabetical Songs list to the song you're trying to find. The only problem with that is that you might have hundreds, if not thousands, of songs loaded onto your phone. Searching through that whole list doesn't sound like a lot of fun. Instead, once you're in the Songs list, just start typing part of the name, and matches will automatically appear (see Figure 7-9). When you find the one you want, tap it.

Figure 7-9: Searching for a song in the Music application.

This technique works in many applications that come with the Pre and also in many third-party applications that you'll download from the App Catalog, but refer to the documentation for the application in question. Depending on the app, there might be other ways to search, too.

Chapter 8

Managing Your Contacts

. . . .

. . . .

*I*n the old days, life was simple when it came to finding someone's phone number or address: You carried around a book of phone numbers with you, or maybe you had a Rolodex on your desk or a shoebox full of business cards. That was all you needed to get a hold of everyone you'd ever need to talk to, plus maybe a small handful of numbers for close friends and family that you'd just memorize. Later on, things started to get a little more advanced, and those business cards became entries in an old-fashioned electronic organizer with a tiny black-and-white display. Life was good!

Life has gotten a little more complicated since those days, though. You likely have contacts stored in all sorts of places: an address book in your Exchange account at work, friends on your Facebook account, and e-mail addresses you've accumulated through the years in Gmail. Suddenly, you realize that the information you used to keep safely in one place is scattered across the Internet! You don't want to have to choose between syncing your device with one source of contact information or the other — but how do you choose?

The good news is that you don't have to choose. You're about to witness one of the most powerful aspects of the Pre's organizational capabilities — its contact management — which centers on what Palm has dubbed *Synergy*. With Synergy, your Pre can to dig through contact information (no matter where it might be), figure out what data overlaps, and reconcile it all into a single address book. In other words, if you work with Joe Smith, you "friended" him on Facebook, and you talk to him on AOL Instant Messenger (AIM), that probably means you have information about him spread across at least three different services on the Internet. Your Pre is smart enough, though, to figure out that Joe Smith in your Exchange address book is the same Joe Smith on Facebook — and then link all that information (plus the AIM account for Joe Smith) to a single contact stored on your phone.

Even better, because all this information is linked to your Palm Profile account, you can't lose it — and if you have to change Pres or change to another webOS device in the future, all of your contact information will transfer. (Read all about your Profile in Chapter 2.) Long gone are the days when changing phones meant a whole weekend spent toiling away re-creating your address book.

In this chapter, you'll read all about creating and managing contacts. And, more importantly, you'll discover that if you already have contacts through another service, odds are very good that you won't have much work to do here because the Pre will know how to automatically add those contacts for you. And we all like less work, don't we?

Getting Started with Contacts

Because contacts are central to so much of what you can do with the Pre — making calls, sending e-mails, instant messages, text messages, and so on— you'll interact with them in many applications on your phone. Fortunately, the Pre Contacts application is your one-stop place where you can add, edit, delete, and manage all your contact information.

The Contacts application is so important and so frequently used that it appears by default on the Quick Launch toolbar so that you don't need to go all the way into Launcher to access it. Look for it at the bottom of the screen in Card View or Launcher, or by dragging your finger up from the Gesture area to display the Quick Launch toolbar no matter what app you're using. (Of course, if you moved Contacts off the Quick Launch toolbar and into Launcher, you'll find it in Launcher, instead.)

The first thing you need to do to start managing your contacts is to create an account. You do this the first time you open the Contacts application. You can always add accounts later. (Don't worry; it's super simple — and I discuss it later in this section.)

Setting up your very first account

The very first time you open Contacts — and each time you open it after wiping your Pre's memory or getting a new Pre and logging into your Palm Profile account, as you'll do here — you'll be given the option to add a Contacts account (see Figure 8-1). You don't have to add an account; the choice is entirely yours. Here's a quick take on what this means:

✔ **If you do add an account:** Your Pre will automatically pull in contact information from this account so that it's available right from your Pre. For most types of accounts, you'll also be able to add new contacts that synchronize back to the account, too, so they're available when you use the account elsewhere (say, on your desktop PC).

✔ **If you don't add an account:** You'll start with a clean slate; your phone might include some pre-entered contacts for your network's customer support line, but you won't have any of your personal contacts automatically loaded for you. You'll be able to add new contacts, which will be stored on your Palm Profile so that they're not lost if you lose, replace, or erase your phone. But if you use Gmail, for example, you won't get the benefit of new contacts created on your phone being made available from your Google account as well.

Figure 8-1:
You're prompted to add a new account the first time you open Contacts.

Unless you don't use any Google contacts, or Exchange or Facebook accounts, odds are very good you'll want to add at least one of these to your Pre to make the process of getting your all-important contact information onto your phone a whole lot less stressful. If you have more than one account that you'd like to add, don't worry; you'll be able to do that momentarily, but you have to start with just one.

If you've already added an account in the Calendar or Email applications, Pre will have automatically set it up for you in Contacts as well.

If you don't want to add an account (you can do so later if you change your mind), tap Done. If you do want to add an account now, follow these steps:

1. **If you see buttons for different account types listed on the screen (Google, Facebook, Microsoft Exchange, and so on), tap the button for the type of account you wish to add. If you don't see these buttons, tap Add An Account, and then tap the button for the account type you want (see Figure 8-2).**

Figure 8-2:
Choose
the new
account
type to add.

2. **In the screen that opens, enter your e-mail address and password for this account (see Figure 8-3).**

3. **Tap Sign In.**

   Depending on the type of account, your Pre might need additional information to connect to it, such as the location on the Internet of your Exchange server. If so, you'll be asked for it now.

   After all the necessary information has been entered, the Pre connects to your account and begins downloading contacts from it. You will see a notification at the bottom of the screen letting you know that the Pre is syncing accounts.

There is also a Sync Now button that you can press at any time to make your Pre sync your account.

The amount of time it takes to download all your contacts from an account will vary greatly depending upon your connection speed, the type of account, and the number of contacts that you have stored on it. Don't be alarmed if your entire address book doesn't show up right away!

Figure 8-3:
Enter login
details
for each
account so
your Pre
can access
the contact
information.

Adding additional accounts

Part of the magic of Pre is watching it expertly handle multiple sources of contact information and shuffle them all into a single application. If you have more than one account — say, a Gmail and a Facebook account — you'll probably want to add them both.

After you add your first account, Contacts doesn't ever automatically prompt you to add an account again (unless you wipe your phone's memory). Instead, you'll do the following:

1. **With Contacts open, tap the Contacts menu in the upper left of the screen.**

2. **Tap the Preferences & Accounts menu item.**

   A new screen opens where the settings for Contacts are configured (see Figure 8-4). I walk you through all these setting in detail later in the chapter.

3. **Scroll down to the bottom of the screen and tap the Add an Account button.**

4. **Tap the button for the type of account you wish to add.**

   A new screen appears, prompting you for your login information for this account.

5. **Enter the e-mail address and password to log in to this account.**

6. **Tap Sign In.**

   Your account has now been added and will begin synchronizing to your Pre immediately.

Figure 8-4:
The
Preferences
& Accounts
screen.

Viewing Contacts

The main view of Contacts is simply a list of all the contacts you have stored on your Pre. By default, your contacts' names are ordered by last name (you'll find out how to change that later in the chapter), and blue divider bars help group contacts whose last names start with the same letter. Check it out in Figure 8-5.

Searching your contacts list

To search for a contact from the list, just start typing the name or company of the person you're looking for. A gray bar appears at the top of the list that shows you what you typed so far, and the right side of the bar shows how many contacts in your list match what you typed. As you type, the list of contacts grows shorter as it filters to show only the names and companies that match your entry.

 After you enter a search term, you can clear the entire term by pressing and holding the Backspace key on the keyboard for about one-half second and then releasing. *Note:* Pressing it more quickly than that deletes only a single letter.

 Although searching from Contacts works great, keep in mind that you can also conduct contact searches from Pre's Universal Search capability, which is even easier to use in some circumstances because you don't need to be in Contacts to use it. Universal Search is covered in Chapter 7.

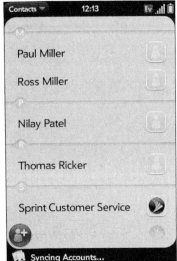

Figure 8-5:
The main
Contacts
screen.

Looking at a contact's details

To see all the details for a contact, just tap the contact (in the main list) that you want to see. The contact's card appears, showing only details that have been filled out. Blank fields are hidden until you edit them; I cover editing later in the chapter. You can see a sample contact card in Figure 8-6.

Each detail appears inside a button-like outline, and many of these details can be used to perform actions simply by tapping them. For example

- ✔ **Phone number:** Besides the obvious capability to place a voice call by tapping a contact's phone number, there's a bonus feature here. Tap the small SMS button on the right side to immediately start composing a new text message to that number.

- ✔ **E-mail address:** Tapping an e-mail address starts composing a new e-mail and automatically puts the selected address in the To field.

- ✔ **IM address:** By tapping an IM address, you'll open the Messaging application, just like tapping the SMS button to the right of a phone number would. In this case, though, you'll be sending your message using an IM account.

- ✔ **Street address:** Need to find an office or a friend's house on a map? No problem — tapping a street address detail in a contact card will take you out to Google Maps and center the requested address on the screen.

    You don't have to have the GPS capability enabled to use this feature.

- ✔ **URL:** You can associate Web site addresses (URLs) with contacts; tapping one of these will simply open the Web application (which you can read about in Chapter 10) and take you to the address.

Phone number

Contact name

Click SMS to send a text message.

Figure 8-6:
A contact
card.

Street address   Associated URL

E-mail address

Synergy in action

Because your Pre might be pulling in contacts from multiple accounts, you
might expect that you'd end up with multiple entries in the contact list for
the same people — one entry for each account that you added. It turns out
they don't, though, and that's where the Synergy technology comes into play
to weed out the duplicates and collect everything under one heading.

In Figure 8-7, for example, I added two different Google accounts to this
phone, and a contact named Paul Miller appears in both. How can you tell
from looking at this? You'll notice that Ross Miller has just a single picture
icon to the right of his name, but the icon for Paul Miller is a "stack" of
pictures. That's Pre's way of letting you know that the Paul Miller contact
that appears on the phone — the Synergy contact — has been automatically
collated from two or more sources.

This contact comes from more that one source.

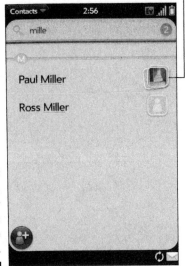

Figure 8-7:
Paul Miller
appears
in multiple
accounts.

By looking at an individual contact card, you can see exactly what accounts are providing the information for the contact:

1. **Tap a contact with a photo stack icon to the right of the name.**

   The contact's card opens. Notice that the photo stack has a number next to it (see the top of Figure 8-8), which is the number of accounts from which information is being pulled.

2. **Tap the gray bar at the top of the contact's card where the name, title, company, and photo stack all appear.**

   Below the gray bar, one line appears for each source contact that was used to create this combined Synergy contact on your phone. The icon on the left of each line indicates the type of account (Google or Facebook, for example). To the right of that, you see the name, title, and company for that contact as they appear in that account. On the right side, you see the contact's picture on that account. *Note:* If there is no picture for a particular account, you'll see a generic picture here.

As shown in Figure 8-8, the line with bold text indicates the *primary profile:* the information that Pre uses for your contact's name, title, company, and picture. This is an important thing to know because these details can vary significantly between accounts: You might normally refer to your buddy by his full name, for example, while he calls himself by a nickname in his Facebook profile. You'll see how to change the primary profile for a contact in the next section.

Primary profile

Figure 8-8:
View
accounts
from which
this Synergy
contact was
created.

Linking and unlinking contacts manually

While you're looking at the list of accounts used to create a Synergy contact on the Pre, check out the Link More Profiles item at the bottom of the list. This can be used to manually tie contacts together when Synergy doesn't quite get it right (which can happen, for example, if you call the same contact by a nickname in one account and by their real name in another). Think of it like rubber-banding two business cards together. Here's how to do it:

1. **Open a contact and tap the gray bar at the top.**

    The list of *contributing accounts* (that is, accounts that have this contact) will be displayed in a list below the gray bar.

2. **Tap Link More Profiles.**

    You return to the list of all contacts.

3. **Tap the name of the contact you want to link to this one.**

And that's it! You've effectively merged these two contacts. You return to the list of contributing contacts for this contact, and the contact you just selected has been added to the list.

Here's a potential gotcha, though: The second contact you selected was made the primary profile when you did the linking. This means that the name, title, company, and picture for the new merged contact — the information that shows in your main contact list — will all come from it. What if you want to use the details from the *first* contact instead? No problem:

1. **In the list of contributing contacts for this contact, tap the contact whose information you want to use; refer to Figure 8-8.**

2. **In the pop-up that appears (see Figure 8-9), tap Set as Primary Profile.**

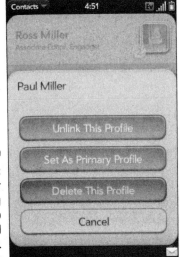

Figure 8-9:
Options for contributing contacts to a merged contact.

If you later decide that you want to keep these two contacts separate, unlinking them is easy:

1. **In the list of contributing contacts for the contact you wish to break apart, tap the contact you want to unlink.**

    If you're dealing with only two contributing contacts in the merged contact, selecting the specific contact that you want to unlink might seem like an unnecessary step. If you have three or more contributors, though, you can see why it's done this way because you could end up just "peeling off" one contributor and leaving the remainder of the merged contact intact.

2. **Tap Unlink This Profile.**

    The selected profile will be broken off from the contact, becoming a separate contact in your Contacts list.

Adding, Editing, and Deleting Contacts

If you manage your contacts exclusively through a service like Google Contacts on your PC, it's possible that you'll never actually add a new contact from your Pre directly. Because the Pre continuously synchronizes all of the accounts you have it connected to, any new contacts that you add (or edit or remove) through your Google, Facebook, or Exchange accounts will automatically update on your Pre as well.

Adding a new contact

For most of us — even if we do 95 percent of our contact management from the comfort of a PC screen — there'll be an occasional time when we actually meet someone, and we want to enter some critical information about this new contact on the spot:

1. **With the main contact list showing in Contacts, tap the New Contact button in the lower left of the screen (see Figure 8-10).**

   A blank, editable contact card appears.

2. **After you fill out the fields you wish (any fields can be left blank that you wish), tap Done in the lower left to save the new contact.**

Figure 8-10:
Add a new contact manually.

Sprint Customer Service

Syncing Accounts...

New contact

Take a closer look at the fields that are available when creating a contact:

✔ **Name:** The contact's full name. Enter it as you'd say it — first name followed by last with no commas. If you need to enter in more specific details about a name (say, a middle name or a suffix), you can tap the Name Details menu item from the Contacts menu, which will give you five data entry fields: Prefix, First Name, Middle Name, Last Name, and Suffix.

✔ **Account:** The small button on the right side of the Name field lets you choose which account this contact should be created on (see Figure 8-11). If you want it to "live" on your Google account, for example, choose Google. If you choose Palm Profile, the contact will be accessible only from your Pre (and other devices that use Palm Profiles). Regardless of where you choose to create it, your Pre will be able to use it and synchronize with it.

Figure 8-11:
Available
accounts
for saving
your new
contact.

You cannot add new contacts to Facebook. Think of it as a read-only service that your Pre can use.

✔ **Job Title:** The contact's title at her company, if applicable.

✔ **Company:** The company that the contact is associated with. This field is searched when you start typing a search term from the main contact list, so it's a useful field to have filled out when possible.

✔ **New Phone Number:** An additional phone number for this contact. Contacts can have as many phone numbers as you need. When you add a phone number, a button appears to the right of it that lets you choose the type of number by tapping on it (mobile, work, fax, and so on).

You don't have to mess with formatting phone numbers with parentheses or dashes — the Pre will do that for you! Because the Pre knows you're entering numbers here, you also don't need to bother holding down the Orange key that's usually required to key-in digits.

✔ **Set a Ringtone:** Set a special ringtone for this contact by tapping this button and choosing a ringtone from the list. That way, you'll know who's calling without even looking at the phone.

✔ **New Email Address:** Like with phone numbers, you can add as many e-mail addresses as you like, and each one can have a type set for it (home, work, or other) by tapping the button at the right side of the text that displays the name of the number type in it.

✔ **New IM Address:** This is the IM username (sometimes called the *screen name*) that the contact uses. You can add many of these from many different services, including AOL, Yahoo!, Google, and MSN.

✔ **New Address:** In the rare event that you can't accomplish something over e-mail, you might have to *actually* mail one of your contacts one day — and when that happens, this field is ready to assist. You can add multiple addresses per contact and choose a type for each one by tapping the box in the upper right of the text. By tapping the lowercase i symbol in the lower right, you can enter in individual portions of the street address separately — city, state, Zip code, and so on.

✔ **New URL:** You can have one or more Web addresses associated with the contact.

✔ **Reminder:** Have you ever said, "I need to tell so-and-so something the next time I talk to her?" Well, the Reminder feature was made for you, and it's hands-down one of the coolest features of the Pre! Enter text into the Reminder field, the next time you interact with the contact on your phone, whether by voice or text, a Reminder notice pops up on the bottom of the screen. Press notice to see the contents of the Reminder.

✔ **Notes:** This is a freehand notes section. Enter whatever you like — don't be shy.

✔ **Birthday, Spouse, Children, and Nickname:** If you're trying to keep track of hundreds of clients, it can be almost impossible to remember who has the daughter named Kris and who has the son named Chris. These fields help you remember those random details about a contact that you wouldn't be able to otherwise.

Editing an existing contact

Editing a contact is essentially the same as creating a new one. The only major difference is that details are already filled out for you:

1. In the contacts list, tap the contact you wish to edit.

The card for this contact opens.

2. **When the card for this contact opens, tap the Edit button in the lower left of the screen.**

   This will make all fields of the contact editable. Just tap the fields you wish to edit and make your changes.

3. **When you're satisfied with your changes, tap the Done button in the lower left of the screen.**

   You return to the read-only view of the contact.

Deleting a contact

If you decide you're no longer friends with your chemistry lab partner from high school (I understand; it happens), maybe you want to delete the contact from your Pre. Here's how:

1. **Open the contact you wish to delete.**

2. **Tap the Contacts menu in the upper left of the screen.**

3. **Tap the Delete Contact menu item.**

4. **If you're sure you wish to go ahead with the deletion, tap the Delete All Profiles button.**

Rest assured that tapping Delete All profiles deletes just this one contact and not all contacts.

Making Contacts More Accessible

Between the Contacts application and Pre's fantastic Universal Search capabilities that I discuss in Chapter 7, it might seem like your contacts can't get any quicker or easier to dial in a hurry — but they can (in a couple of ways, actually).

Speed dial

Pre's speed dial capabilities are unparalleled by any regular phone. Why's that, you ask? Unlike most phones which typically have nine assignable speed dial numbers, virtually all Pre keys can be set to dial a number of your choosing when held down! (E is an exception because it doubles as the 1 key, which is universally recognized as the standard voicemail access button.) To set a speed dial, follow these steps:

1. **Open the contact to which you wish to assign a speed dial key.**

2. **Tap the Contacts menu in the upper left of the screen.**

3. **Tap Set Speed Dial.**

   A new screen opens with all this contact's phone numbers listed.

4. **Tap the contact's phone number that you wish to assign to a speed dial key.**

   A list of available speed dial keys appears in a list.

5. **Select the speed dial key you wish to use for this contact by tapping its entry in the list on the screen.**

   You can select a key that's already assigned to another contact. If you do, you'll receive a warning and be given the option to reassign that key to this contact instead (see Figure 8-12).

Now, whenever you hold down the assigned key for a few seconds — and you're not editing text — this contact will be dialed.

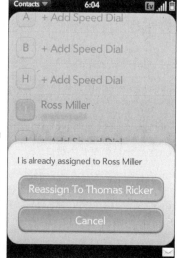

Figure 8-12:
You can reassign an existing speed dial to a different contact.

Adding a contact to Launcher

Speed dial is great for the fastest possible access when you need to call someone, but what if you just want fast access to *all* of a contact's information? Maybe you find yourself texting or e-mailing someone more than you're calling them, and in that case, speed dial isn't the best option. In this case, you might want to drop a frequently accessed contact right into Launcher alongside your applications:

1. **In the Contacts application, open the contact you wish to place in Launcher.**

2. **Tap the Contacts menu in the upper left of the screen.**

3. **Tap Add to Launcher.**

4. **In the screen that appears, type the text you want to appear below the contact icon's name in Launcher.**

   By default, the contact's first name and last name are used.

5. **Tap Add to Launcher again.**

   The icon is immediately added to Launcher although it won't be shown to you right away; you have to go into Launcher to see it. It can be moved and manipulated just as any other application icon. One extra item of note: If the contact has a picture, that will show up as the icon.

To remove a contact's Launcher icon, return to the contact's card, go to the Contacts menu, and tap Remove from Launcher.

Preferences & Accounts

There aren't too many settings to be concerned with in Contacts (refer to Figure 8-4), but here's a quick glance at what's available. To get there, go to the main contacts list, open the Contacts menu, and then choose Preferences & Accounts.

- ✔ **List Order:** Choose how contacts are sorted in the main list. Options are First Name, Last Name, Company & First Name, and Company & Last Name. The default is Last Name, which will be the logical choice for most users.

- ✔ **Accounts:** View what accounts are currently linked to the Contacts application. Palm Profile will always be there, but beyond that, it depends on what additional accounts you've configured. By tapping any of these accounts, you can see how many contacts they each contain, change your login information (important if you change your Google password, for example), and remove the account altogether by tapping the Remove Account button.

  Removing contact accounts takes a surprisingly long time, so make sure you don't need to have access to your contacts for up to an hour or so before attempting to remove an account.

- ✔ **Default Account:** This setting determines the default account to add new contacts to. You can change this while creating the new contact if you wish, as discussed earlier in the chapter.

✔ **Sync Now:** Immediately synchronize all your accounts with the Pre, rather than waiting until the Pre thinks it needs to be done. If you know you've just made a lot of changes to the contacts in your Google account, for example, and you want to get the changes onto your Pre as quickly as possible, tap Sync Now to make it happen.

✔ **Add an Account:** As discussed earlier in the chapter, you can tap this button to add a new contact account to the application.

And just like that, the Pre magically whips all your contacts into one magic hat! It might not support every service you use, but Palm will be adding more, so keep your eyes peeled. You can also find out about syncing your Pre directly to Outlook on your PC in Chapter 16.

Chapter 9

Planning Your Day with Calendar

*O*ne of the great things about the Pre is how simple it is to manage your contacts. (Check out Chapter 8 for more on the Contacts application.) And as an added bonus, your Pre can help you organize contact information from different sources, because of the technology that Palm calls *Synergy.* It should come as no surprise, then, that Contacts isn't the only place where you'll find Synergy at work — it plays a big role in the Calendar application, too.

Just like your contacts, your daily schedule is something that you probably have segmented into at least two distinct categories — work and personal — and for the most part, you probably want to (or have to) store and manage those schedules using different tools. For example, you might use an Exchange account at work, where both your office calendar and your corporate address book are housed. When you leave the office, though, you might use Google Calendar to keep track of your bustling social life.

It's not uncommon for smartphones and other electronic organizers to be able to synchronize using only a single source of calendar information (if they can even synchronize with calendars at all), which means that you're stuck choosing between managing your job or your personal life from the convenience of your pocket. More often than not, folks choose to manage their work schedule on their device out of necessity — and what's the fun in that (literally)?

The Pre uses Synergy to allow you to manage and synchronize multiple calendars at once, and it does it so seamlessly that you don't even have to know or care about which schedule information is coming from which source (unless you really want to) — it's just there. Seeing everything you need to do and everywhere you need to be from the moment you wake up to the moment your head hits the pillow has never been so easy.

In this chapter, you'll see how to add, view, and manage your calendar information on your Pre, regardless of the source of that information. You'll also see how to create new calendar events, set reminders, and change how the Calendar application looks and behaves. Making your dentist appointment on time, though. . . . Well, I'm afraid you'll still have to manage that one on your own.

Starting Up Calendar

Calendar is such a frequently used application on the Pre that Palm includes it on the Quick Launch toolbar, which means you can access it simply by tapping an icon at the bottom of the screen in Card View or in Launcher, or by dragging your finger upward onto the screen from the black gesture area below the screen (see Chapter 3 for a refresher on this gesture and others) while you're in any application and letting go while the Calendar icon is selected.

 If you moved the Calendar icon off the Quick Launch toolbar (you're not big on schedules — trust me, I can understand), you'll find it in Launcher with the rest of your applications. Just press the Calendar icon to open it. And if you'd like to customize your Quick Launch toolbar, now that I've brought it up, head back to Chapter 3 for details.

Opening Calendar for the first time

The first time you open Calendar, you're given the option to add an account. Just like accounts in Contacts, though, you don't have to do this — the choice is yours.

- ✔ **If you do add an account:** You'll be able to see all Calendar entries from that account. With the exception of Facebook, you'll also be able to create new events and save them to those accounts, which means that you'll be able to see these events from other machines right on your Pre. If you add an Exchange account, for example, and you use Outlook to access Exchange from your PC, any new events that you add to your Pre (and save to your Exchange account) will be seen in Outlook as well.

- ✔ **If you do not add an account:** You will start with a completely empty calendar. You'll still be able to add events, but they'll only be saved to your Palm Profile. In other words, they won't be visible or accessible anywhere but your Pre and other devices that are connected to your Palm Profile. If you don't use Google Calendar, Facebook, or Exchange (or don't wish to connect any of them to your Pre), this is the way to go.

If you previously added an account somewhere else on your Pre (in the Email or Contacts applications, specifically) that also supports calendars like Google or Exchange, the Calendar application will have automatically added it for you so that you don't have to add it again right now.

To proceed without adding an account, just tap Done, and you'll be taken straight into a new blank calendar. Proceed to the "Viewing Your Calendar" section later in the chapter to start using how to use this screen.

Creating your Calendar account

If you wish to add an account now (you can add one, but you'll have a chance to add more later — you'll see how in the next section), follow these steps:

1. **Tap the account type that you wish to add (see Figure 9-1).**

   You can choose from Google, Facebook, and Exchange.

Figure 9-1:
You can associate an account with Calendar the first time you open it.

2. **On the following screen, enter your e-mail address and password for this account into the text fields.**

3. **Tap Sign In.**

   Depending on the account type, you might be asked for some additional details at this point. With Exchange, for example, you'll need your account's mail server, domain, and username, all of which your Exchange support team can provide to you. After you enter these details, tap Sign In again at the bottom of the screen.

When you finish adding the account, your Pre will automatically begin synchronizing data from it and pulling calendar information down to the phone (see Figure 9-2). The amount of time this process takes can vary greatly depending on the number of calendar entries you have, the speed of the data connection that your phone is connected to, and the type of account being synchronized. However, you can use Calendar immediately while the process occurs: You don't have to wait for it to finish before using the application.

Figure 9-2:
The account you just added is now being synchronized.

Sync indicator

Adding Calendar accounts

Perhaps you didn't add an account the first time you opened Calendar, and you changed your mind, or perhaps you need to add a second (or a third, or a fourth!) account into the mix. Either way, no problem:

1. **In Calendar, press the Calendar menu in the upper left of the screen.**

2. **Tap the Preferences & Accounts menu item.**

   The Preferences & Accounts screen opens, which I cover in depth later in the chapter.

3. **Scroll down to the bottom of the screen and tap the Add an Account button.**

   A list of available account types appears.

4. **Tap the type of account you wish to add.**

   At this point, you go through the same process to set up the account that I describe in the preceding section. After you're done and you tap the Sign In button, your Pre will start synchronizing the new account you added. In just a few minutes' time (or less), you'll have a combined view in Calendar that includes this new account.

Some applications that you download to your Pre (more on that in Chapter 15) can add additional accounts to the Calendar application as well. One example of this is Flixster, which can indicate movie times right in your Calendar. These types of accounts are automatically created when the application is installed and automatically removed when the application is removed.

Viewing Your Calendar

The first thing you'll see whenever you launch Calendar is the Day view for today's date, but there are actually three different ways to look at your schedule: Day view, Week view, and Month view.

To switch between the three views, tap one of the three buttons at the bottom of the Calendar application (see Figure 9-3). You'll find out more about each of the three views in the next few sections.

Figure 9-3:
Switching
between
Calendar
views.

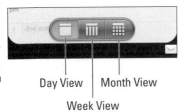

Day View | Month View

Week View

Choosing the accounts and calendars you want to see

By default, Synergy works to show you a combined view of all your calendar entries, regardless of the account from which they come, but you can filter your view so that you see only a single account. Some account types, such as Google, support multiple calendars. For these, you can view only one calendar at a time when you don't have your Pre set to show all calendars.

Regardless of which calendar view you are using, you'll see a dark gray bar across the top of the application. This bar tells you what time period you're looking at. For example, in Week view, it might read Week of Jul 12, 2009; while in Day view, it would read Sunday, Jul 12, 2009.

There's a special exception in Day view for the current day: It'll read Today.

To the right of the time period, you'll see a button that reads ALL by default. To display only a specific calendar, follow these steps:

1. Tap the ALL button.

A menu appears of all the calendars that the Pre has available. To the left of each calendar, you'll see the color used to indicate that calendar's entries. That way, it's easy to identify where each entry is coming from. Because certain types of accounts can have multiple calendars within them, the calendars are grouped by account, and you'll see a blue bar above each group with the group's name.

A total of eight colors are available on the Pre for color-coding your calendars from different accounts (which should be enough for pretty much everyone — and if you have more than eight calendars, we're curious when you have a chance to sleep!). The Pre will randomly assign a color to each account, but if you want to change it, see the "Configuring the Calendar Application" section, later in the chapter.

2. Tap the name of the calendar you wish to view. Or, if you wish to view all calendars, tap All Calendars.

Changing days, weeks, or months

Regardless of whether you're in Day view or Week view, there's a very easy way to change the day or week that you're viewing:

- ✔ **To go back a day or week:** Swipe your finger toward the right side of the screen.
- ✔ **To go forward a day or week:** Swipe your finger toward the left side of the screen.

When changing days, weeks, or months in the Calendar, make sure that you're swiping your finger on the screen, not on the black gesture bar below the screen.

When in Month view, the action is slightly different:

- ✔ **To go back a month:** Swipe your finger toward the bottom of the screen.
- ✔ **To go forward a month:** Swipe your finger toward the top of the screen.

Alternatively, you can go to a specific day via the menu:

1. Tap the Calendar menu in the upper left of the screen.

2. **Tap the Jump To menu item.**

   A pop-up window appears, prompting you to enter a date. If you want to go straight to today's date, tap Go To Today now; otherwise, continue these steps.

3. **Fill out the month, day, and year you wish to navigate to by tapping each of the three fields and selecting the appropriate values.**

4. **Tap Go to Date.**

You can also go to a specific day using the gray date bar at the top of the screen:

1. **Press the gray date bar.**

   A pop-up window appears where you enter the date of your choice (this is the same pop-up window you get when choosing the Jump To... menu item described in the previous set of steps).

2. **Fill out the month, day, and year you wish to navigate to.**

3. **Tap Go To Date.**

Tapping a second time on the Day View, Week View, or Month View button at the bottom of the screen returns you to the current day, week, or month, respectively, so don't be worried about losing your place while moving around the app.

Day view

You'll probably find yourself using Day view (see Figure 9-4) more than any other because it shows you a detailed, hour-by-hour breakdown of today's (or any day's) schedule. Week view and Month view are good for longer-term planning, but Day view is the meat and potatoes of the Calendar application.

Below the gray bar at the top of the screen, any all-day events you have are displayed. Below that, events with fixed start and end times are shown in a timeline from midnight to midnight. The all-day and timed events are actually in separate sections of the screen that can be scrolled independently, which is convenient because your all-day events will never leave the screen as you scroll around to see what you have going on during the day.

Collapsing the view

The problem with viewing a 24-hour day one hour at a time is that, well, in all likelihood, you don't have stuff scheduled for most of those 24 hours. (And if you do, you're in serious need of a vacation.) The Pre does something very smart to make these big gaps between events more readable: It collapses the empty space like an accordion (see Figure 9-5) and lets you know how much time is compressed with a label at the right side of the screen.

Figure 9-4:
Day view.

First event   Gap

Figure 9-5:
Two events
separated
by a 13-hour
gap in Day
view.

Second event

If you want to expand the accordion, tap it. To collapse it again, find the label
that shows how much time is in the gap (you'll find it halfway between the
two closest events) and press it.

Viewing individual events

To see all the details of an individual event in your calendar, just tap the event's item in your calendar. A new screen opens (see Figure 9-6) showing everything you need to know about the entry, from top to bottom:

✔ **The name of the event and the account on which it is stored**

✔ **The date, time, and duration of the event**

✔ **The location of the event**

This can be any text, but to get the most use out of the application's capabilities, this should be in a format that Google Maps can understand (such as a street address or the name of a restaurant or other business).

✔ **Whether the event is set to repeat itself in Calendar**

✔ **Whether there's a reminder set for the event**

✔ **Any other notes about the event**

This can be anything you like.

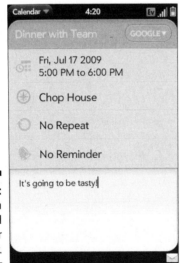

Figure 9-6:
Viewing an
individual
calendar
entry.

You can search for the location entered for this event on Google Maps right from this screen:

1. Tap the Calendar menu in the upper left of the screen.

2. **Tap the Map Location menu item.**

Google Maps immediately opens in a new card and searches for the text listed in the location field for this event.

The color of the bar at the top of the screen (right below the status bar) when viewing an individual calendar entry corresponds to the color-coding for all the calendars from different accounts available on your Pre.

Week view

Week view in Calendar (see Figure 9-7) is a good for getting a glance at how busy you are this week. However, because you can't see any words on individual entries, you'll still have to go into Day view to get a better idea of what each event is. Fortunately, there's a really easy way to do that:

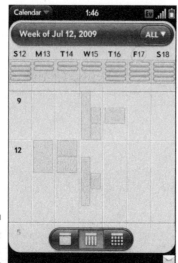

Figure 9-7:
Week view.

1. **Find the day whose details you want to see.**

2. **Tap anywhere within the column representing that day.**

   You're taken to the Day view for the requested day.

Today's date will be circled in blue (as in Figure 9-8).

Month view

Finally, Month view is — you guessed it — a bird's-eye overview of how your month is shaping up (see Figure 9-8). It can't give you the level of detail of Day (or even Week) view, but by tapping on a date square, you're taken to the Day view for that day. In both Week view and Month view, today's date is circled in blue.

Figure 9-8:
Month view.

Adding, Editing, and Deleting Calendar Entries

Depending on how you use your phone, you might just choose to do all your Calendar event creation and editing on something with a little more horsepower like a PC. If you do, you can skip this section altogether. Pre automatically synchronizes your calendars so that you always see the latest and greatest entries in Calendar. Otherwise, though, you'll be pleased to hear that creating, managing, and removing entries right from your phone couldn't be easier.

Adding a calendar entry

To add an entry to your calendar

1. **Open the Calendar application and go to Day view (as described in the previous section) for the day of the event you want to add.**

2. **Scroll to the time of the event and tap the area to the right of the event's time (see Figure 9-9).**

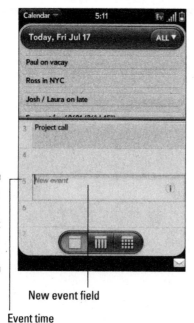

Figure 9-9:
Adding a
new event
to the
calendar.

New event field

Event time

3. **Type the name of the event, using the keyboard.**

   If the time and duration of the event are both roughly correct and the event is attached to the account and calendar to which you want it attached (or you don't really care in this case), you're all set adding this event and can go ahead and press Enter. Otherwise, continue with these steps.

4. **Press the lowercase i icon to the right side of the new event.**

   The Event Details screen appears.

5. **Fill out the fields you'd like.**

6. **When you're done, perform a back gesture (see Chapter 3 for details on this and other gestures) on the gesture area below the screen.**

To create an all-day event, tap the date/time detail within the Event Details screen and enable the All Day Event check box.

Changing the calendar to save this new entry

Your default Calendar account is automatically chosen for new entries that you create on your Pre, but you can save new events to a different calendar if you like, by following these steps:

1. **While in the Event Details screen for an event, tap the button to the right of the event name at the top of the screen.**

   This button will show the name of a type of Calendar account (Google, for example). At first, this button should be showing the name of your default Calendar account.

2. **Choose the account (and calendar, if applicable) where this event should be saved.**

Setting up a recurring event

You can cause an event to be repeated on a regular basis. While setting up the event

1. **Tap the No Repeat button.**

2. **Choose the type of recurrence you would like.**

   Regardless of the type you choose, the recurring event is at the same time as the first. If you choose Custom, a new screen appears where you will have significant control over the date scheduling of the event, but the time is still fixed to the first time setting.

   After you choose a recurrence type, the No Repeat button will change to reflect the recurrence type that you selected.

Setting up a reminder

What good is an appointment if you can't remember that you have it? Maybe that's a rhetorical question — but for the purposes of this conversation, assume that you actually want to remember the events on your schedule! That's not a problem at all:

1. **Press the No Reminder button.**

2. **In the pop-up that appears, choose how long of a lead time you'd like on the reminder by tapping the corresponding menu item.**

   After you choose a reminder type, the No Reminder text on the button will change to reflect the type of reminder that you set up.

At the time of the reminder, you'll receive a notification at the bottom of the Pre's screen, just like you would for many other applications on the phone.

Modifying and deleting entries

You modify and delete calendar entries the same way you view their details: by tapping the entries in Day view. While you're viewing an entry's details, all details are editable as if you were creating a new entry: Just tap the detail you want to change to modify it.

To delete an entry, follow these steps:

1. **Tap the Calendar menu in the upper left of the screen.**

2. **Tap the Delete Event menu item.**

   You're presented with a pop-up message confirming that you wish to delete this event (see Figure 9-10).

Figure 9-10: Are you sure you want to delete this calendar entry?

3. **Tap Delete.**

If you delete a calendar entry from a non–Palm Profile account (Google or Exchange, for example), remember that your changes and deletions affect the entries on your account and all other computers and devices that use the account— not just your Pre!

Configuring the Calendar Application

As I discuss earlier in the chapter, the Preferences & Accounts screen is where you set options for Calendar. You can get to it by selecting the Preferences & Accounts menu item from the Calendar menu.

Take a look at the settings available:

- **First Day of Week:** This determines the first day on the left side of Week view in Calendar. The default setting is Sunday, but some locales use Monday.

- **Day Start and End:** Bold horizontal lines in Day view delineate work hours, and these lines can be adjusted by changing these times.

- **Default Event Reminder:** If you prefer to have reminders set for all your calendar entries, you can choose default reminders (separate ones for timed and all-day events) here so that they're selected automatically when you create a new event.

- **Event Reminders — Play Sound:** If you want a sound to play in addition to the notification at the bottom of the screen when an event reminder goes off, make sure this option is set to On.

- **Default Event Duration:** When you tap to the right of the timeline in Day view to create a new event, it automatically creates a one-hour event. You can adjust the length of this default event by changing this value.

- **Accounts:** These are the Calendar accounts set up to use with the application. By tapping an account, you get a few options (note that Palm Profile can't be removed):

  - *Calendar Color:* For each calendar within this account, tap this item to change its color.

  - *Display in All Calendars View:* If you wish to hide certain calendars from displaying even when the Calendar application is set to ALL in the calendar display selection, you can change this value to Off.

  - *Change Login Settings:* If you changed the username or password for this calendar, tapping this button allows you to update your login information on the Pre.

  - *Remove Account:* If you wish to remove this account from Calendar altogether, press this button.

- **Default Calendar:** This selects the calendar to automatically use when creating a new event. Press it to select a different one.

✔ **Sync Now:** Calendar changes on your accounts and on your Pre will be synchronized immediately. You typically won't have to do this (the Pre does it automatically) unless you made specific changes that you want to be updated to an account immediately.

✔ **Add an Account:** As mentioned earlier in the chapter, tap this to add another calendar account to the Pre.

Part IV
Staying Connected and Playing with the Pre

The 5th Wave   By Rich Tennant

"He seemed nice, but I could never connect with someone who had a ring tone like his."

In this part . . .

*E*arlier chapters in the book walk you through — shall we say, more "work-related" features? — of the Pre. Don't get me wrong. It's interesting stuff, and webOS makes it as easy and fun as it can possibly be. Still, every once in a while, you want to kick back with some Web surfing, some music, or some videos, right? That's where Part IV comes into play.

In Chapter 10, you'll find out how to use the Pre as one of the most convenient (yet powerful) Web browsers you've ever seen. From there, you'll start to explore the Pre camera in Chapter 11 and see how to browse videos in your Pre's memory and on the Internet. Chapter 12 gets you to that new pizza place downtown in a hurry, thanks to your Pre's built-in navigation capabilities. In Chapters 13 and 14, I show you how to use the Pre as one of the best portable music players around, and you'll find out how to check out TV and streaming radio when you get bored of the tunes you have stored in memory. When you finally get tired with all that stuff (trust me, it'll take a while), I'll show you how to go find new applications to download and use.

Chapter 10

Browsing the Web

*N*ot long ago, phones simply weren't expected to be able to browse the Web. Instead, some publishers produced mini-pages — WAP sites — that lacked much of the glitz, glamour, and shine of a traditional Web site in exchange for making Web pages small enough to transfer quickly onto a cell phone (with a slow data connection), and that could look right on a small display. Sadly, these WAP sites were few and far between. And even on the off-chance that some of your favorite full Web sites produced mobile versions, they rarely had enough quality content to make them worth your time.

Nowadays, those old-school speed and size concerns have largely vanished. Handsets like the iPhone and the T-Mobile G1 (just to name a couple) have rewritten the rules for how well mobile devices should be able to load regular Web sites — yes, the very same ones you'd view from your desktop computer — and the Pre happily follows suit. Features such as a large, high-resolution touchscreen display, 3G data support, and a fast processor all help make it possible.

In fact, depending upon the phone you used prior to the Pre, it's entirely possible that you've never even tried browsing the Web from your phone. After you start, though, you'll *never* want to go back. It's a whole new world!

On the Pre, your Web browser is known simply as *Web* (easy enough to remember). In this chapter, you'll see how to take advantage of the Web application to browse your favorite sites across the Internet. Who knows — maybe you won't even need a browser on your PC anymore! (Not likely, but you never know.)

Opening (the) Web (Application)

Just like your PC, you'll probably find that you frequently get to the Web on the Pre via a link rather than by opening the browser directly. For example, if someone sends you a link to a Web site in your e-mail, clicking that link starts Web in a new card (that is, in Card View) and take you directly to the site. (Read all about Card View in Chapter 3.)

Alternatively, you can start Web (the Pre app, that is) without clicking a link: Just go to Launcher and tap the Web icon. The first screen you'll see is your Bookmarks page (as shown in Figure 10-1), which gives you quick, one-press access to the pages you set up to appear here. Each tile on the screen is a bookmark. By default, you'll see a few pages that Palm and your network operator have configured for you — such as Facebook, MySpace, and Palm's own site — but they're easy to change. Later in this chapter, I talk about bookmarks and how to change them.

Figure 10-1:
The
Bookmarks
page.

Navigating to Pages and Searching

Palm realized something really interesting about the way we all use the Web: We search for things just as much as we navigate directly to sites, if not more. Using that knowledge, Palm integrated page navigation and searching into a single function so that you can do the both exactly the same way. You don't need to remember which box or menu item to go to — it's all in one place.

Going places and finding things the easy way

Palm has taken navigating and searching one step further: You don't even need to go anywhere to type in your Web address or search term! You can just start typing, no matter where you happen to be within the Web application. As long as you aren't in the middle of filling out a text box on a Web site, Pre will know that you want to search for something or go somewhere. This method works both from the Bookmarks page and also from any Web page that you happen to be viewing.

Give it a try to see how it works:

1. **Open the Web application, if you haven't already done so.**

2. **Start typing a Web address (or search term) of your liking.**

   You won't see any box on the screen in which to start typing the address or search term — you just start typing.

   For example, if you want to go to wiley.com, just type **wiley.com**. If you want to search for Web pages about dogs, just type **dogs**.

While you type, a box appears at the top of the screen where you can see what you're typing, as shown in Figure 10-2. Directly below that, a menu appears where the Pre will try to finish the term for you, using Google or Wikipedia entries. You can either select one of these options (as shown in Figure 10-2), or you can keep on typing the rest of your search term. If you select either of the top two menu items that appear directly below the text box you're typing into, you can search for what you just entered via Google or Wikipedia, respectively. Additionally, if any Web sites in your bookmarks or your history match what you typed, they'll appear directly below the search options.

As you probably already noticed, Web is designed to cater to the lazy bum in all of us. You don't have to enter your addresses into any particular place, there's no need to differentiate between addresses and searches, and it automatically gives you search options as you type. When you do enter an address, though, the Pre takes you straight to the Google Maps entry for it by default. And if you enter a search term, the Pre brings up the Google search results for that term. *Note:* If you want to search the term in Wikipedia, you still have to press the Wikipedia option in the menu that appears while you type.

Further your search options

Your search term displays here.

Figure 10-2:
The Pre
offers
options as
you type
your search
term.

A bookmark or history hit

Seeing where you are

Usually, all you see in Web is the Web page that you're browsing. That's a good thing; after all, the Pre screen is only so big, so it makes sense to maximize the space that's available to browse. Occasionally, though, you might want to get your bearings and find out the name, address, or both of the page you're on:

1. **While on a Web page, swipe your finger on the screen in a downward motion, as if you want to scroll the page up. Continue swiping and scrolling the page up until you're at the top of the page; then swipe once more.**

   You'll uncover a hidden address bar above the top of the page (see Figure 10-3) that tells you the name of the page or site that you're viewing.

   The bar displays only when you're viewing the Web application in portrait mode. In *landscape mode* (that is, when you're holding the phone so that it's wider than it is tall), you won't see it.

"Hidden" address bar

Figure 10-3:
The address
bar.

2. **To view the page's Web address instead of its name, tap once on the bar.**

   The address will display where the name just was. It's highlighted automatically, which makes it easy to copy (if you want to send the address in an e-mail, for example).

When you're done using this super-secret address bar, just swipe your finger upward to scroll the Web page down, and the bar disappears at the top of the screen. You can actually think of this bar as being "attached" to the top of the page — and always available by scrolling to the very top.

Moving between Pages

Quite often, you'll just need to view a single Web page that you received in an e-mail or a text message, or your browsing session will be "linear" — that is, you'll just progress from one link to the next without going back and forth. Just like the features you have available to you on a desktop browser, though, Web makes it easy to go back and forth through your browsing history so that you're never more than a press or two away from revisiting the sites and pages that you browsed earlier.

Forward, backward, and reload

At the bottom of every page you visit, depending on the situation, you'll find either two or three buttons that "float" over the page (see Figure 10-4).

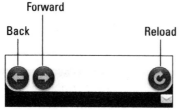

Forward

Back

Reload

Figure 10-4:
The Back,
Forward,
and Reload
buttons.

- ✔ **Back:** Tapping this takes you to the last page you visited immediately before the one that you're viewing. If this is the first Web page you've viewed in this browser window, pressing Back takes you to the Bookmarks page.

- ✔ **Forward:** This button appears only if you previously tapped the Back button in the current browsing session and you're not on the final page you navigated to. If you think of your Web browsing session as a line, the Forward button makes a whole lot of sense — it simply takes you forward on this line, and Back takes you back. It works exactly the same way as the Forward button in a browser on your PC.

- ✔ **Reload:** Pressing this button requests the current page again over your data connection, which is convenient if you're looking at sports scores or stock prices, for example, and you want to see the very latest information available. Occasionally, pages might not load completely — say, if your data connection is momentarily lost — in which case, this is a convenient way to try loading it again.

- ✔ **Stop:** When a page is in the process of loading, the Reload button toggles to a Stop button, identified with an X in the middle of it. Tapping the Stop button halts the Web application in its tracks and prevents it from loading any more data on the current page. *Note:* This could leave you with a partially loaded page that doesn't have all its information. When this happens, the Stop button toggles back to a Reload button, and you can load the stopped page again by tapping Reload.

While a Web page is loading and the Stop button is displayed, you'll notice a blue ring around the edge of the button. This is the Web application's estimate of how much of the current page has loaded! For example, if the blue ring goes halfway around the button, the application estimates that 50 percent of the page has loaded. Thanks to technical limitations in how the World Wide Web works, this progress bar can't be perfectly accurate, but it should give you a pretty good idea of how much more waiting you have ahead of you.

History

What was that great contemporary French recipe Web site you visited yesterday? Do you remember? If you don't, I can't say that I blame you — it happens to me all the time — but fortunately, your Pre has a better memory than you do!

Viewing the History page and navigating to recently viewed Web pages

The History page gives you quick, one-press access to a chronological list of pages that you recently visited. To access it from anywhere in the Web application

1. **Tap the Web menu in the upper left of the screen to open it.**

2. **Choose the History menu item.**

   You see the History page (see Figure 10-5), which is simply a list of Web pages that you've been to recently. Your most recent visits appear at the top, listed in chronological order with the oldest visits at the very bottom. To select an entry and immediately navigate to it, tap it briefly with your finger (as you would any other link), and the site will open.

Clearing your browsing history

Say you're giving your Pre to your buddy, and you don't want him to know that you spend your entire day reading about hamsters or model trains. What do you do? If you want to clear you history so that the list of your recently viewed Web pages is no longer visible or accessible, do the following:

1. **While viewing the History page, tap the Web menu in the upper left of the screen.**

2. **Choose the Clear History menu item.**

   All your history items are removed and are no longer visible or accessible.

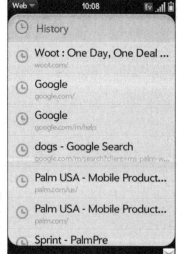

Figure 10-5:
The History
page.

You won't be warned or asked for confirmation when you choose the Clear History command, so make absolutely sure that you wish to delete your list of all recently viewed Web pages before you do so!

Don't call 'em tabs: Managing cards

If you've used a Web browser in the past several years, you're probably familiar with the concept of *tabs,* which allow you to open many Web pages at once in the same window. This is convenient for when you need to rapidly move back and forth between a few different pages and forms, or if you have a few favorite sites that you always like to keep open and readily accessible.

The Pre uses a similar concept, but instead of having tabs within the Web application, you simply get a new card for each page you have open, just as if it were a new application. (See Chapter 3 for more on cards.) You can manage each card just like you would any other card on the Pre, and you can move between open pages by pressing the Center button below the screen to get to Card View and then moving between cards. This means that open Web pages can be intermixed with applications, which you might not like. Remember, though, that because you can reorder open cards, you still have a way to keep pages grouped together if you like.

To open a new Web page in a new card and keep the current page open, follow these steps:

1. **While the page you wish to keep open is displayed onscreen, tap the Web menu in the upper left of the screen to open it.**

2. **Choose the New Card menu item.**

   A new card immediately opens, and you're taken to it. The first thing that you see is the same thing you see when you're opening the Web application from the launcher — the Bookmarks page.

   The page you were just on a moment ago is still open, just on another card.

3. **To return to the originally open card, press the Center button below the screen to get to Card View, scroll left and right through the cards until you see the page you wish to open, and then tap on the page.**

Moving around the Page

After you get the hang of getting between pages using the Web application, it's time to master getting around in a page How do you see the whole page, or get in close so you can see a piece of it really well? How do you select links to navigate to them? Well, as luck would have it, you've come to exactly the right section to find out!

Scrolling and selecting links

Web does an excellent job of displaying Web pages in exactly the same way as you'd see them on your laptop or desktop computer. Because the Pre screen is much smaller than the screen on your PC, though, you can't see as much stuff onscreen at one time. That means that you want it to be as easy as possible to quickly scroll through pages because you'll be doing a lot of it — and, fortunately, scrolling couldn't be any easier.

Scrolling around pages

As I discuss in the earlier section, "Seeing Where You Are" (on exposing the hidden address bar), you scroll a page down by swiping your finger up along the surface of the screen. Conversely, you scroll up a page by doing the opposite and swiping your finger down along the screen. This might sound backward, but in practice, you'll find it's very natural. (If you've used an iPhone, you'll notice that scrolling works in exactly the same way.)

Similarly, scroll left by swiping your finger to the right, and scroll right by swiping your finger to the left. Practice this motion a few times, and you'll have it down pat.

Navigating links on a page

Navigating links on a page couldn't be much simpler. Just press briefly on a link, which appears in underlined blue text on the page, to open it. As I describe earlier in the chapter, new links that you open will replace the page you're viewing by default, but you can open links in new cards if you prefer by holding down the Orange key and the Symbol key on the keyboard while you select the link with your finger.

Zooming in and out

Because most Web sites are designed for screens that are much larger than the Pre, you'll find that you have to scroll around quite a bit to see everything that you need to see. Another trick is to zoom in and out. When you're zoomed out, you can get a bird's-eye view of the page. After you used that to identify the area of the page that you want to look at more closely, zoom right into that specific location. On a desktop Web browser, this is usually a cumbersome trick involving a menu item or a key combination, but on the Pre, all you need is a finger or two to zoom around.

There are two distinct types of zooming in Web, and you'll discover both here. The first is a *smooth scroll,* which you can control very precisely with the movement of your fingers. Try these steps:

1. **With a Web page open, place two fingertips on the screen (see Figure 10-6).**

Figure 10-6:
Zooming
with two
fingers on a
Web page.

2. Slowly move your fingertips apart.

As your fingers move, you'll notice that the page zooms in so that you can see everything closer and more clearly. The center of the zoom is the halfway point between your two fingertips.

3. Slowly move your fingertips back together.

This time, the page zooms back out at the same rate that it zoomed in. Again, the zooming action will be centered midway between your two fingers.

If you don't need that level of control over how closely zoomed in the page is, here's another way to zoom in the Web application that's just a little bit faster:

1. With a Web page open, double-tap — that is, tap twice quickly in the same place — with a single finger somewhere on the page.

As if by magic, the Pre zooms right in to the area you just tapped. It tries to take a guess at how much it should zoom in, but it won't always get it exactly right. You can still manually control your zoom level from here by using the two-finger method described in the preceding step list.

2. Double-tap again.

When you're zoomed in on the page, a second double-tap will tell the Pre that you want to zoom back out.

Changing screen orientation

You'll find that sometimes it's easier to view a Web page in *landscape orientation* (the screen is wider than it is tall) than how you normally hold and use your Pre (in *portrait orientation,* when it's taller than it is wide). To switch to landscape — like in many other applications on the Pre — just physically rotate your Pre 90 degrees clockwise or counter-clockwise. The phone automatically detects that it has been rotated and will rotate the Web page to match (see Figure 10-7).

When and how you use landscape orientation on the Web is strictly a matter of taste, but because the Pre keyboard will be sideways, you'll probably find it a little tough to enter text into Web forms (or enter new addresses or search terms) while in landscape mode. It's a fun challenge, though!

Figure 10-7:
Viewing a
Web page in
landscape
orientation.

Bookmarking Pages

Most likely, you have favorite Web sites that you visit on a regular basis (plus, perhaps, a few that you *don't* count among your favorites, but you have to visit anyway — say, for your job or to pay bills online). The Pre makes it easy to get to those pages quickly.

The Bookmarks page (refer to Figure 10-1) comes up each and every time you start the Web application, and whenever you open a new card. It presents a graphical *tile view* of your bookmarked sites that allows you to quickly choose a site by sight instead of having to read titles or Web addresses — that is, each bookmark is presented as a small tile in a grid.

Adding a new bookmark

To add a new bookmarked page, follow these steps:

1. **With the Web page open that you wish to bookmark, tap the Web menu in the upper left of the screen to open it.**

   The menu won't be visible at the upper left of the screen if you're viewing a Web page in landscape orientation. Rotate your Pre so that the long side is being held upright when you need to access the Web menu.

2. **Choose the Add Bookmark menu item.**

   A new screen opens (as in Figure 10-8) allowing you to edit the name of the page as it appears in your Bookmarks page and the graphical representation of the page.

Figure 10-8:
The Add
Bookmark
screen.

This graphical representation is a little tricky because the Bookmarks page doesn't use it. The tile that you see on the Bookmarks page will always just be a little piece of the page taken from its upper-left corner. Instead, the graphic you choose here will be used for the bookmark's icon. This icon displays on the Bookmarks organization page and when you're adding a page to Launcher (both of which I cover in the following sections).

Now to assign this graphic to the icon.

3. Touch the graphic in the center of the upper portion of the Add Bookmark screen.

A new view opens, as shown in Figure 10-9. The Web page that you're adding as a bookmark will appear in the background, and the high-lighted square area in the center represents the area that will be used for the graphic. You can scroll around and zoom in and out of the page just as you would if you were viewing it normally. Use these functions to get just the right area inside the square. For example, you might want to center the Web site's logo in icon or a memorable picture from a Web site.

4. When you're happy with the graphic, tap the Done button at the bottom of the screen.

5. **(Optional) To modify the name or the Web address of the bookmark, tap the Title or the URL field, respectively, and use the keyboard to make changes.**

You probably don't want to mess with the URL field unless you have a very specific reason to do so! The Web application automatically fills out this field for you when you press the Add Bookmark menu item, using the address of the page currently displayed. In most cases, it should be correct.

6. **Tap the Add Bookmark button.**

And you're done! Your new bookmark now appears in the Bookmarks page every time you open the Web application.

Reorganizing and deleting bookmarks

By default, any new bookmark that you add automatically becomes the first bookmark in your collection, which means that it appears at the upper left of the Bookmarks page. If you want to reorder these — or delete any of them — there's another screen for that.

Reordering a bookmark

Follow these steps to change the order of your bookmarks:

1. **While viewing a page, tap the Web menu in the upper left of the screen.**

2. **Choose the Bookmarks menu item.**

   You're taken to a new organization screen where you see a list view of all your bookmarks (see Figure 10-10).

3. **Pick up the bookmark by pressing an item with your finger until it changes to a lighter gray color.**

4. **Drag the bookmark, keeping your finger on the screen the entire time, to the new location where you'd like it to be.**

5. **Drop the bookmark by taking your finger off the screen.**

   This method probably feels familiar to you if you've ever reorganized cards in the Card View because it works basically the same way.

Figure 10-10:
The Bookmarks organization screen.

Deleting a bookmark

To delete a bookmark, place and hold your finger on the bookmark in the list and then swipe to the left or right. Two buttons appear: Delete and Cancel. Press Delete to continue with the removal of this bookmark, or Cancel to back out.

You can't delete a bookmark from the Bookmarks page that displays when you first start the Web application — it needs to be done from here.

You can also delete all your bookmarks in much the same way that you would use to clear your history:

1. **Tap the Web menu in the upper left of the screen.**

2. **Choose the Clear Bookmarks menu item.**

Be careful! Just like on the History screen, pressing Clear Bookmarks immediately deletes all your bookmarks without first asking you for confirmation!

Changing a bookmark's details

By pressing the lowercase i icon that appears at the right side of each bookmark entry (refer to Figure 10-10), you'll be taken back to the bookmark editing screen. Here, you can modify the graphic, the name as it appears in your Bookmarks page, or the Web address itself. When you're done, tap Save Bookmark, or tap Cancel to throw away your changes.

Adding Web pages to Launcher

For Web pages that you visit frequently, maybe a regular bookmark is enough. But what about pages that you visit really, really frequently? For those pages, you have another option: You can actually add the page right to Launcher. That means you won't even need to come into the Web application first to get to the page because it has an icon all its own in Launcher, which you can tap to take you straight to the page. You can treat this Launcher icon like you would any other, organizing it however you like.

Adding a page to Launcher

The process for adding a page to Launcher is very similar to that for adding a bookmark:

1. **With the Web page open that you want to create a Launcher icon for, tap the Web menu in the upper left of the screen.**

2. **Choose the Page menu item.**

   This opens a submenu with two items: Add To Launcher and Share.

3. **Choose the Add to Launcher menu item.**

   The bookmark editing screen opens, where you can set the page's graphic, change its title, and change its Web address. Keep in mind that both the graphic and the title will appear in your Launcher, so make sure they're exactly how you want them to be.

Removing pages from Launcher

To remove a page's icon from Launcher

1. **Open Launcher and go to the page where the icon you want to remove appears.**

2. **Hold down the Orange key on the keyboard and briefly press the icon with your finger.**

   Two buttons appear at the bottom of the screen. To remove the icon, tap Delete; to back out and leave the icon as-is, tap Cancel.

Sending Web Pages to Others

Occasionally, you might come across a Web page so incredible, so awesome, so amazing, that you just *have* to send it to a friend or a co-worker. No sweat:

1. **With the page that you want to share showing onscreen, tap the Web menu in the upper left of the screen.**

2. **Choose the Page menu item.**

   This opens a submenu with two items: Add To Launcher and Share.

3. **Choose the Share menu item.**

   The Email application opens and automatically starts a new e-mail with a link to the page attached in the body (see Figure 10-11). And here's the cooler part: Pre will also attach an image of the Web page so your recipient can get a preview of the page without having to open it in her browser. (Of course, you can remove this attachment if you prefer — head on over to Chapter 5 for more on that.)

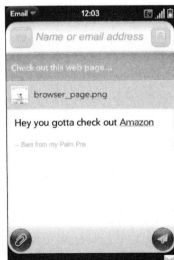

Figure 10-11:
Sharing a
Web page
over e-mail.

Setting Web Preferences

Unlike some browsers, there are just a small handful of settings that you can configure in the Pre Web app. To open the Preferences screen

1. **From within the Web application, tap the Web menu in the upper corner of the screen.**

2. **Choose the Preferences menu item.**

   A new screen opens (see Figure 10-12) where you can see all the settings that are available to you:

   - *Block Popups:* Some Web sites might attempt to automatically open new browser windows. (Odds are that you've experienced this on your PC's browser a few times.) By default, this is set to Yes, which means the Pre will block sites from opening these. I recommend leave this enabled; otherwise, you might find that new cards are opening without your permission.

   - *Accept Cookies:* Many (if not most) Web sites use *cookies,* which are tiny files that are stored within your browser and allow the site to keep track of who you are. This enables many features on sites (shopping carts, for example), and they should usually be left enabled unless you're browsing a specific site where you don't wish to be tracked.

   - *JavaScript: JavaScript* is a programming language that Web sites often use to perform tasks that they wouldn't be able to do otherwise — everything from performing calculations to automatically changing appearance based on buttons and links that you press and a whole lot more. JavaScript is so powerful, in fact, that modern sites rely on it to function properly, so you probably want to leave it enabled unless you have a specific reason to turn it off.

   - *Clear History:* Earlier in this chapter, I discuss how to clear your history from the History screen, but you can also do it from here. Just tap the button.

   - *Clear Cookies:* Clearing cookies will delete all the cookies stored in the browser, which means that any sites that have placed cookies there will lose track of who you are. You won't typically want to do this unless you have a specific reason to do so.

   - *Clear Cache:* Web automatically stores some images and files right on the Pre while you browse around the Internet to make it faster to reload pages in the future. This storage area is called *cache.*

If you want to force the Pre to reload all pages from scratch to ensure that you're seeing the latest and greatest information available on the Web, you can completely empty the cache by tapping the Clear Cache button.

As a test, try going to all your favorite Web sites right now to see how they look and perform on the Pre. I bet you'll be delighted by how well they do.

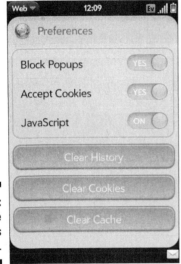

Figure 10-12:
The
Preferences
screen.

Chapter 11

Working with Photos and Videos

*A*re you a shutterbug? Maybe you're the type of person who can't leave home without the trusty point-and-shoot (or if you're *really* into photography, the trusty SLR or dSLR, three different lenses, and an external flash unit that's bigger than your head). Even if you don't usually find yourself regularly pulling out a camera to capture that special moment, though, you might find yourself snapping a few more photos now that you have the Pre by your side.

In this chapter, you'll discover how to take, manage, and share pictures. You'll also get a quick tour of the Photos application's sibling — Videos — which, you guessed it, is where you'll go to play videos on your Pre.

The Pre Camera

Until recently, cameraphones simply weren't expected to take very good pictures. The camera modules on these handsets were little more than novelties — last-minute additions that were just good enough to let you take tiny, fuzzy pictures that you could send to a friend as a multimedia message. They looked alright on a tiny phone screen, sure, but you wouldn't even dream of e-mailing the photo to someone and expect them to be able to use it as a PC wallpaper. The quality just wasn't high enough.

More recently, the optics and sensors in phone cameras have started to improve by leaps and bounds. They've gotten so good, in fact, that the picture quality produced by some of the better cameraphones on the market is all but indistinguishable from a typical dedicated compact camera. Just as modern smartphones have started to replace dedicated portable music players, they've started to replace dedicated cams, too!

Happily, the Pre has developed (pun intended) a reputation for having one of the better cameras in its class, capable of producing some truly stunning pictures in the right conditions. For starters, the Pre camera uses a generously sized 3MP sensor, which means that it can produce images large enough to make great-looking 4" x 6" or 5" x 7" prints.

The camera also sports an LED flash that you can use to brighten dark scenes. And although it does lack true autofocus, the Pre optics feature "extended depth of field," which means that you can keep more of what you see through the viewfinder in focus at once. (Translation: you'll get sharper pictures, and you'll get them more frequently.) Plus, the exclusion of autofocus means that you're able to take pictures more quickly because the phone doesn't have to refocus the image between shots.

The Pre camera creates JPEG images, which are a predominant standard across the Internet. If you download Pre camera images, you won't have a problem opening them regardless of what computer or OS you use. The JPEG format is a very efficient standard that doesn't take up a lot of memory, so you'll be able to store several thousand images at once in your Pre's memory! *Caveat:* Image storage is shared with music and any data that your applications store, so your actual available image storage space will vary.

Managing your memory

Although your Pre comes with a vast 8 gigabytes of storage space, it's definitely possible to fill it up with music, pictures, e-mail attachments, and files from various applications that you've installed. The process for deleting things on your Pre varies from application to application, but how do you find out if you need to make room to begin with?

The secret lies in the Device Info screen. Go to Launcher and tap the Device Info icon (found on the third page of Launcher icons, unless you moved it). Here, you'll see a bunch of statistics about your Pre's battery, memory, hardware, and software. Look for the line that read `Available`. This is the amount of free storage space you have. If this number is getting low (say, less than 100MB or so), you might want to consider deleting images and other files to make some room.

And after you capture your photos, Pre offers a great application to manage them — aptly named Photos — which you can use to share your shots with the world through common picture-sharing sites.

Using Camera

Nothing like the present to get started. To take a picture on the Pre, begin by opening the Camera application (which I just call Camera from here on):

1. **Open Launcher.**

2. **Find and tap the Camera icon.**

   Camera opens in a new card, and the camera on the back of the Pre is activated. From the lens on the back (as shown in Figure 11-1), you'll immediately start to see onscreen what the camera sees.

Flash

Lens

Figure 11-1: The Pre camera lens and flash.

Unlike almost every application that you use on the Pre, you'll notice something very interesting about Camera: It takes up the entire screen. That means that when you're using the phone's camera, you won't be able to see the status bar or your notifications because Palm wants to give you as much space as possible to use as a viewfinder. You can, however, still get the Quick Launch toolbar to show by dragging your finger up from the Gesture area — see Chapter 3 for details.

There's not a whole heck of a lot to using Camera. Figure 11-2 shows the interface in portrait (taller than wide) orientation:

✔ **Image center:** This plus-sign marker indicates the center of the image that you'll be taking. Use it to help you align your shots.

Don't assume that the center also helps determine what part of the shot is in focus. Pre is fixed-focus.

✔ **Flash mode:** This indicator shows how the LED flash on the back of the Pre will be used during the next photo that you take. Three modes are available:

- *On:* The flash will fire, regardless of ambient light conditions.

- *Off:* The flash will *not* fire, regardless of ambient light conditions.

- *Auto:* Pre decides whether to fire the flash, depending on how much light you have around you. This is the default mode.

   On

   Off

   Auto

✔ **Shutter release:** This big, green button is hard to miss — it takes a picture. Just tap it to take your shot.

✔ **Photo roll:** This icon looks like a stack of photos, and the photo on top is the last one that you took. Tap this to go to the Photos application to access your collection of photos. More on this a bit later in the chapter.

Setting the flash

As I mention in the preceding section, the flash is set to Auto mode by default. Generally speaking, you want to leave the flash in this mode because your Pre has a pretty good idea of when it does and doesn't need the flash to help illuminate your picture.

If you want to override the Pre's setting, though, it's easy: Tap the Flash mode icon once to activate the flash, and tap it a second time to turn it off. Tapping it a third time returns you to Auto mode. You can see what each icon looks like in the preceding list.

Image center

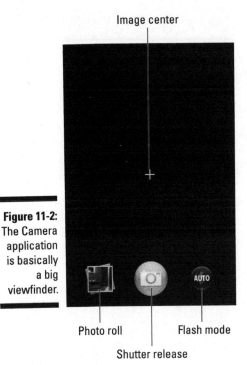

Figure 11-2:
The Camera
application
is basically
a big
viewfinder.

Photo roll   Flash mode

Shutter release

Taking a picture

To capture what you see onscreen (while Camera is open, of course), simply
line up your shot and then press the big green Shutter Release button. If
the flash is set to On (or if it's set to Auto and the phone decides that it's
needed), that icon will light up briefly while the picture is taken.

Instead of pressing the green Shutter Release button on the screen, you can
also press the spacebar on the keyboard to take a picture.

If you want to take a picture that's longer than it is wide — more like a
traditional camera — just turn your Pre sideways. It'll detect that you
changed orientation, and all the controls on the screen will automatically
rotate to accommodate you (see Figure 11-3). You can actually hold the Pre
right side up, sideways facing left or right, or upside down — it'll know what
you've done and compensate accordingly!

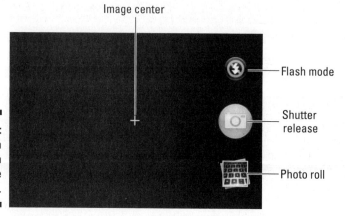

Image center

Flash mode

Shutter release

Photo roll

Figure 11-3: The camera controls in landscape mode.

Seeing your pictures

After you take a picture, the Photo Roll button updates to show the photo you just took; this photo sits at the very top of the "stack" of this button. You can see this button in Figure 11-2.

Tapping the Photo Roll button now launches the Photos application and takes you straight into the Photo Roll, which is a special category where pictures you've captured with the camera are stored. You'll learn everything you need to know about Photos (and viewing and managing your shots) in the next section.

Tapping the Photo Roll button launches Photos in a new card. To return to taking pictures, you'll need to go back to Card View: Using the Pre's Center button, navigate back to the Camera card (or launch it again via Launcher).

Viewing and Managing Photos

As I mention, you can access Photos directly from Camera by tapping the Photo Roll button, but here's a more traditional way to get in there: Just tap the Photos icon in Launcher.

Albums

If you open Photos from Launcher, the first thing you'll see is the list of all photo albums on the phone, as shown in Figure 11-4. You can also think of these albums as folders or categories — they're simply ways of organizing your photos into groups. To the right of each album's name is a preview of some of the images along with a total image count for that particular album.

You can create your own albums by connecting your Pre to your computer, which you'll discover how to do in the upcoming section, "Transferring images to and from your computer."

An album can't have subfolders.

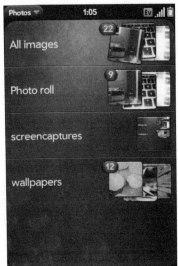

Figure 11-4:
The photo albums on your Pre.

By default, you'll see these albums listed:

- ✓ **All Images:** This album holds every image that Photos could find in your Pre's memory.

- ✓ **Photo Roll:** This album holds photos that you captured using Camera. This is also the album you're automatically taken to when you tap the Photo Roll button in Camera.

- ✓ **Messaging:** If you save an image that you received in an e-mail or a multimedia message to your Pre, it's filed in this album.

- ✓ **Wallpapers:** Here, you can find a collection of high-quality images that the Pre comes with that make perfect *wallpapers* (which appear behind cards in Card View).

In addition to these standard albums, Figure 11-4 shows another: Screencaptures. This special album is created whenever you take a picture of your Pre screen, which might be useful if you want to send a friend a picture of a cool application you have, for example. To do that, hold down the Orange, Symbol, and P keys. (Here's a little secret: That's how I took most of the pictures in this book!)

To see the pictures contained within a particular album, just tap the album name. You'll be taken to a grid of image *thumbnails* — small, square versions of every image available in that album. See an example in Figure 11-5.

Figure 11-5:
A grid of
images
contained
within an
album.

Working with individual images

From the list of thumbnails, tap any image to be taken to a full-screen view of that image; see Figure 11-6). Swipe your finger left and right across the screen to move between images in this album without having to return to the thumbnail grid. If you rotate your Pre left, right, or upside down, the image rotates and resizes accordingly.

At the top of the image is a gray bar. This bar will go away after a moment, but you can touch the image briefly to bring it back. In the middle of the bar are the album name and the position of this image within that album. This bar allows you to do a few cool things, too, which you'll see over the next few sections.

Deleting an image

If you have a shot you're not happy with, or you're doing a little housekeeping to free up some memory, removing an image from your Pre is simple:

1. **Tap the trash can icon on the right side of the gray bar that appears at the top of the image.**

   A confirmation message appears.

2. **Tap the Delete button to go through with the deletion or Cancel to back out of it.**

Share   Album Image   Trash

Figure 11-6:
Looking at
an image
full-screen.

If you don't have this image saved somewhere else (like your PC), the image is gone forever when you confirm the deletion by tapping the Delete button, so make sure you really want it to disappear — there's no Undo!

Using and sharing images

By tapping the Share icon in the upper-left corner of the gray bar that appears at the top of images, a menu will appear from which you can do a number of things:

✓ **Assign to Contact:** Use this to associate the selected image with a contact in your Contacts list.

   a. *Tap Assign to Contact.*

   You're taken to your Contacts list.

b. *Select a contact by tapping it.*

You're taken to a screen where you decide what portion of the image should be used for the contact. You can see what I mean in Figure 11-7, where the photo has a white square imposed on it.

Contact images must be square.

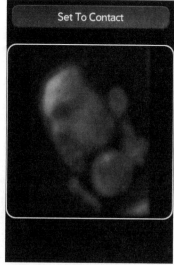

Figure 11-7:
Setting a
contact's
image.

c. *Use your fingers to move around, zoom in, and zoom out to make sure only the portion of the image that you want to use for the contact is contained within the white line.*

d. *When you're satisfied with the picture to be used, tap the Set to Contact button to assign the photo to the selected contact.*

✔ **Set Wallpaper:** Tap this to use the current image as your Pre wallpaper. This is the image that appears behind cards when you're in Card View.

✔ **Share via Email:** Tap this to automatically launch the Email application and starts a new e-mail with the current image attached. All you need to do is choose a recipient and then fill out a subject line and body — you're ready to send a message with a photo attachment.

✔ **Share via MMS:** Tap this to launch the Messaging application and start a new multimedia message with the current image attached.

✔ **Upload:** Tapping this takes you to a new screen where you can select a photo-sharing service on the Internet to upload this photo.

To use this feature, you must first have a photo-sharing account set up in Photos, which I cover a little later in the chapter.

You can't edit photos on your Pre — to get rid of red eye, for example. If you need to edit your photos, you need to transfer them to a computer to get the job done. Keep reading to see how.

Too, album names and contents can be modified only by connecting your Pre to a computer. You can't move images from one album to another on the Pre itself — so the bottom line is that you've got plenty of good reasons to connect that cable!

Transferring images to and from your computer

Because your Pre can simply act as a regular USB drive (sometimes known as a *thumb drive*) when you connect it to your computer, moving pictures back and forth between your Pre and your computer is just as easy as moving them between two folders on your hard drive.

Pre can recognize images in the GIF, JPEG, PNG, and BMP formats. Any other format of image that you transfer to the Pre's storage will not be recognized as an image, and you won't be able to view it using the Photos application.

1. **Using the Pre's included USB cable (or an approved replacement), connect the Pre to your computer's USB port.**

   Your Pre doesn't have to be powered on.

   Your Pre asks you what mode you want the Pre to be in while it's connected to the computer. For the purposes of organizing and transferring photos, you want to be in USB Drive mode.

2. **Tap USB Drive.**

   Your computer will automatically recognize your Pre as a new connected USB drive.

3. **On your computer, open the new drive that has appeared on your Desktop (for Macs), Computer (in Windows Vista and Windows 7), or My Computer (in earlier versions of Windows).**

4. **With the drive window open, create new folders and drag images from your computer into them.**

   This creates new albums that are accessible on your Pre the next time you open Photos. Likewise, you can drag images into existing folders on your Pre's drive and drag images out from the Pre and into folders on your computer.

   You can also drag individual images directly into the root of the Pre's disk, but when you do that, they won't appear in any album in the Photos application — they'll only be accessible from All Images.

5. **When you're done transferring photos, eject the Pre's drive from your computer the same as you would any other USB drive.**

   In Windows, right-click the Pre's drive in the Computer/My Computer window and choose Eject. On a Mac, you can drag the Pre's drive to your Trash.

6. **Disconnect the Pre from the computer.**

The only way to add a new folder to Albums is by creating it on a computer and then uploading.

Adding and uploading to a photo-sharing account

If you want to be able to effortlessly upload pictures from your Pre to a public photo-sharing site where your friends can easily see them, you need to first set up a photo-sharing account:

1. **While in Photos, tap the Photos menu in the upper left of the screen while viewing albums or thumbnail grids.**

   The menu does not appear while viewing individual photos.

2. **Tap the Preferences & Accounts menu item.**

   The Preferences & Accounts screen doesn't really have any "preferences" here, per se, but it does offer a list of the photo sharing accounts you have set up, along with a button to add new ones.

3. **Tap Add an Account.**

4. **Choose the type of account to add.**

   At the time of this writing, your choices are

   • Facebook

   • Photobucket

5. **Fill out your username and password in the provided fields and then tap Sign In.**

After an account is added, you can remove it or change the password used to log into it by tapping its item in the Accounts group in the Preferences & Accounts screen.

Now upload a photo to the photo-sharing site you added:

1. **In the Photos application, open the photo you wish to upload.**

2. **Tap the Share button in the upper left of the photo.**

3. **In the menu that appears, tap the Upload menu item.**

   Below the Upload menu item is a list of available photo-sharing accounts that you've added.

4. **Tap the menu item for the account you wish to upload this photo to.**

   You see a message at the bottom of the photo that it's being uploaded; after a moment, the message is replaced with Upload Complete. You can now let your friends know to check out your Facebook or Photobucket account to see your newly uploaded photo.

Watching Videos

Unlike a still photo, your Pre can't capture video using the onboard camera, but you can still enjoy videos that you receive in messages or that were copied to your Pre from your computer while connected via USB cable. To check out all the videos you saved on your phone, you use the Videos application.

The Videos app can play the most popular video formats in use today, including MP4, 3GPP, H.264, and M4V. (If you're not sure whether the Pre will play a particular type of video, it's worthy copying it over and giving it a shot.)

Launch Videos by tapping the Videos icon in Launcher. You'll immediately see a list of all videos that could be found in your Pre's memory. Each item in the list will include the video's name, duration, file size, and a preview image of the video's contents on the right side of the screen.

To start playing a video, tap its item in the list to go to the video player. The video will immediately start playing from the beginning. Controls for the video (as shown in Figure 11-8) will appear briefly at the bottom of the screen before disappearing so they don't interfere with the video you're trying to watch. You can get them back at any time by tapping the screen while the video is playing.

Figure 11-8:
Video controls at the bottom of the screen.

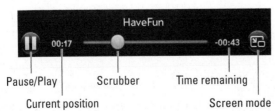

Here are the controls available on the screen:

- **Pause/Play:** Tapping this starts and stops playback of the video.

- **Current position:** This number indicates how far into the video you are, expressed in minutes and seconds.

- **Scrubber:** The *scrubber* is a visual indication of your current position in the video, with the beginning of the video being at the left of the blue line and the end of the video being at the right. The circle on the line is your current position. By placing your finger on the circle and dragging left or right, you can change your current position — a really convenient way to quickly fast-forward or see a scene again.

- **Time remaining:** This is the amount of time remaining in the video, expressed in minutes and seconds.

- **Screen mode:** This button toggles between viewing the video in its original size and fitting it to the Pre's screen.

Videos play only in landscape mode (in other words, with your Pre held sideways). The demo video that is included on the Pre appears to play in portrait mode, but it was actually just recorded sideways so that it would show up that way.

Swiping your finger from left to right across the screen while a video is playing will jump the playback forward by 30 seconds. Swiping your finger from right to left will jump it back by 10 seconds.

The YouTube App for Pre

The Pre also comes bundled with a separate application that is used to watch YouTube videos, which is a source of endless amusement and a great time-waster when you have a few minutes to kill.

To start the YouTube application

1. **Open Launcher.**

2. **Tap the YouTube icon.**

   Unless you moved it, you'll find the YouTube icon on the second page of Launcher.

Lists of videos and searches

You'll first see a list of the currently most-popular videos on YouTube along with some information about each video (see Figure 11-9).

Search bar Video title Viewer rating

Uploading member Duration

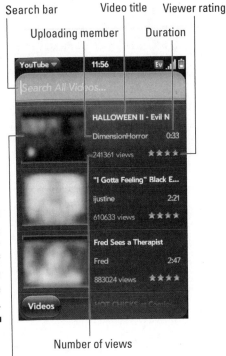

Figure 11-9:
The Popular
view of
videos in
the YouTube
application.

Number of views

Video preview

By tapping the Videos button in the lower left of the screen, you can choose
from different lists of videos:

- **Popular:** The videos that are popular on YouTube at this moment. This
  is the default view.

- **Most Viewed:** A list of videos that have been viewed the most times.

- **History:** A list of videos that you've viewed. You can clear this list by
  selecting this view and tapping the Clear button that appears in the
  lower right of the screen.

You can easily run a search of the entire YouTube database of videos on the
Internet for videos.

1. **Tap the search bar at the top of this screen.**

2. **Enter text that you want to search for.**

3. **Tap the magnifying glass button that appears at the right side of the
   search bar, or press the Enter key on the keyboard**

   When the search is complete, you get a list of videos that match.

Viewing a video's details

By tapping on a video in the list, you'll be taken to a details screen where you can see more information about the video, including a larger preview and the video's full description. Check it out in Figure 11-10. Just scroll down if it goes off the bottom of the screen

Figure 11-10:
Viewing
details
about an
individual
video on
YouTube.

Tapping the More button in the lower left of the screen will bring up a menu where you can choose from

- ✔ **More from This Author:** See a list of other videos that were uploaded by the same person as this video.

- ✔ **Related Videos:** See a list of videos with content that YouTube believes might be related to this video.

Tapping the Share button in the lower right of this screen calls up a menu from which you can send a link to this video in a new e-mail or text message.

Playing videos

To play a video, just press the image of its preview either in the list of videos or in an individual video's details screen. When you're done with the video, perform a back gesture (see Chapter 3 for a refresher on gestures) to return to the screen you were previously on.

Chapter 12

Finding Your Way with the Pre

● ●

● ●

Your Pre contains a GPS chip as well as two applications that use it to help you get where you need to go: Sprint Navigation and Google Maps. I explore those apps in this chapter, along with some third-party apps you can download through the App Catalog to help you find what you need and how to get there.

Getting Around with Sprint Navigation

The Sprint Navigation app on your Pre offers live navigation, providing verbal and visual turn-by-turn instructions to get you from your location to the destination of your choice. Sprint Navigation monitors your progress throughout your trip and even attempts to re-route you if you choose to not follow directions.

If your sense of humor is anything like mine, you might find it entertaining to set a course to a destination you know and then ignore Sprint Navigation to see what it does.

The Sprint Navigation app enables you to find out how to get where you want to go in a variety of ways. You also can save directions to places and then quickly and easily redisplay them. Sprint Navigation uses Location Services; or, if you're out of range of the Sprint network, Wi-Fi to determine where you are so it can help you get where you need to go. Both Location Services and Wi-Fi take advantage of the GPS chip in the phone to determine your current position on the planet.

To load the Sprint Navigation app

1. **Tap the Launcher icon on the main screen of your Pre.**

2. **Swipe from right to left in Launcher until you find the Sprint Navigation app; then tap it.**

   When you first load Sprint Navigation, a Terms of Use agreement appears.

3. **Read and accept the terms to use the application.**

4. **When prompted to allow Location Services to function, tap Allow to use the app.**

5. **A screen appears where you set up login information; supply your first and last names and (an optional) e-mail address.**

   You can change this information later, if you want, by selecting Preferences from the Sprint Navigation menu.

6. **Tap Continue.**

   Sprint Navigation proceeds to log you in and the main screen of Sprint Navigation appears (see the left side of upcoming Figure 12-1). From this screen, you can select a variety of ways to search for directions to a location.

Consider a few examples of how you might search for directions. The method you choose to search for a location doesn't really matter because after Sprint Navigation finds the location and you select it, you follow the same basic procedure to have Sprint Navigation plot a route for you.

Searching for a business

Suppose, for example, that you're out and about and want to pick up a few things at the grocery store on your way home. Your favorite grocery store — the one you always go to — isn't on the way home, but it's a chain store, and you'd like to find the one closest to your current position. Tap Drive To on the main screen and then tap Business. Or, you can tap Search (also on the main screen; left side of Figure 12-1). Either approach gets you to the search screen shown on the right side of Figure 12-1.

Type in the name of the grocery store and then tap the arrow beside the search field, or press Enter on the keyboard.

As you type the name for which you're searching, Sprint Navigation displays common names that contain the letters you have typed; if one matches, you can tap it.

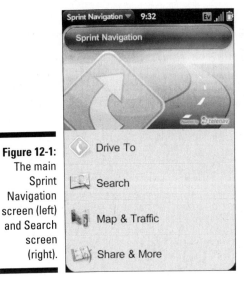 

Figure 12-1:
The main Sprint Navigation screen (left) and Search screen (right).

Sprint Navigation searches for the name you typed and displays a list of matches, sorted by the results that best match what you typed (see Figure 12-2). I'll call these hits the Search Results list. Tap the Sort By button in the upper right of the Search Results List screen to change the order to those closest to your current geographic location or those rated best.

Change your sort here.

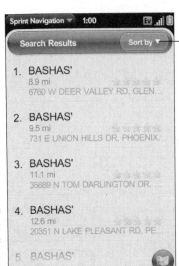

Figure 12-2:
The result of a search.

After tapping a search result to select it, you can tap View Reviews to see reviews others have posted about the selected location or tap Share to send the address to someone else via e-mail or text message.

Sprint Navigation features an address book — My Favorites — that you can use to store addresses. If you plan to be in this neighborhood frequently and want to save the information to your My Favorites list, tap Save. You can then change the name of the entry, after which it's saved to My Favorites, which you can access later by tapping the Share & More item on the main Sprint Navigation screen.

If you tap View Map, Sprint Navigation displays a map showing pushpins that represent the locations of other entries in the search results list (see Figure 12-3). Using the icons at the bottom of the map from left to right, you can hide or display traffic information, see your current location, or return to the Sprint Navigation screen.

Pushpins

Figure 12-3: When you view a map of search results, a pushpin represents each result.

To get directions, tap one of the entries in the Search Results list; Sprint Navigation displays a screen like the one shown in Figure 12-3, where you have several options.

You can use pinch gestures, as described in Chapter 3, to zoom in and out of the map on this screen. If your search result pushpins are too close together, zooming in is a good way to spread them out a bit and make them easier to select.

It doesn't matter what method you choose to search for a location. After Sprint Navigation finds a location, you see a screen like that shown in Figure 12-4.

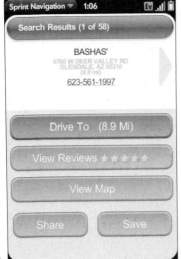

Figure 12-4:
The screen
after you
tap an entry
in a Search
Results list.

To get verbal and written turn-by-turn directions to the destination, tap Drive To. The verbal instructions also warn you of construction and heavy traffic conditions and display an alert in the lower-right corner. Click the alert, and Sprint Navigation will attempt to find you an alternative route to avoid the problems.

On the 3-D map, you'll see your current location, the first direction, the total miles to your destination, and your estimated time of arrival (see Figure 12-5). Each direction remains onscreen until you complete it; the GPS chip in your Pre lets Sprint Navigation know that you've completed the turn, and verbal instructions continue to the second direction.

If you need to hear a direction again, tap the box in the upper left of the 3-D map that contains the direction symbol.

Because your Pre relies on a clear line of sight to GPS satellites to get a good position signal, there may be times when the phone temporarily loses GPS reception while you're navigating. If this happens, you'll see an icon on the screen that looks like a satellite with a red X through it. Don't worry, though, because Sprint Navigation will pick right up where it left off as soon as it can find a signal again. If the lost signal caused you to miss a turn (or three), you'll be rerouted to get back on track automatically.

Tap to hear the direction again.

Figure 12-5:
A typical Sprint Navigation map that appears with turn-by-turn directions.

Tap to view written directions.

To view the written instructions, tap the address at the bottom of the screen. On the screen that appears, tap Trip & Traffic Summary to see the screen like that shown in Figure 12-6. Tap any entry on these instructions to hear verbal instructions associated with the entry you tapped. Using the buttons at the top of this screen, you can check traffic along the route, and you can see an overview map of the directions.

Searching for an airport

This one's really handy. Your Pre can quickly get you directions to the airport — whichever airport you need. Tap Drive To (refer to Figure 12-1) and then tap Airport to see the screen shown in Figure 12-7. Sprint Navigation uses your current GPS location and automatically displays a list of nearby airports. You can select one, or you can type in an airport name or code.

Yes, you can actually get directions to drive from Phoenix, Arizona to Chicago O'Hare airport.

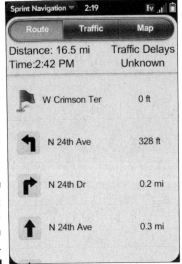

Figure 12-6:
Turn-by-
turn written
directions.

Figure 12-7:
Sprint
Navigation
uses current
location to
display a list
of nearby
airports.

After you select an airport, Sprint Navigation plots a route and displays a 3-D map like the one shown earlier in Figure 12-5, and you hear verbal, turn-by-turn instructions. You can tap the current location at the bottom of this 3-D map screen to view the written instructions for following the route and check traffic along the way. You can also see an overview map of the directions like the one shown in Figure 12-8.

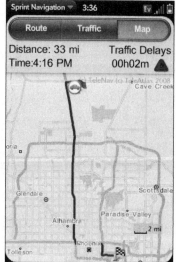

Figure 12-8:
A sample
overview
map of a
route that
Sprint
Navigation
plotted.

Searching for an address

Suppose that you're on your way to meet a friend whose current address is not the one you have stored in Contacts. You could do the following:

1. **Tap Drive To from the Sprint Navigation main screen and then tap Address.**

2. **Fill in the friend's current location to get driving directions.**

3. **On the Find Location screen, as shown in Figure 12-9, type the address information and then tap Submit.**

Instead of typing the address, you can also speak it! Tap Call It In, which will open the Phone application with a number filled out for you. Dial this number by tapping the Call button and follow the voice prompts for dictating your address. After you're done, your dictated destination will appear at the very top of the Recent Places list that you can select when tapping Drive To from the main screen.

Sprint Navigation validates the address and then creates a route.

A 3-D map appears, similar to the one shown earlier in Figure 12-5, and Sprint Navigation begins to give you verbal turn-by-turn directions to the address. On the 3-D map, you can tap the address to view written turn-by-turn directions, and tap any direction to hear it verbally. You also can use the buttons at the top of the screen to view an overview map of the route and check traffic along the route.

Figure 12-9:
Fill in the
address
information.

Tap to enter an address by voice.

When you tap the Traffic button, Sprint Navigation displays information, such as the current speed along various segments of your route (see the left side of Figure 12-10).Green roads are 50 mph or greater; yellow are 30–50 mph, red are crawling along at less than 30 mph, and the speed information for gray roads is unknown.

Caution symbols appear for segments that might pose problems; you can tap a caution symbol to see the details associated with the problem segment (see the right side of Figure 12-10). Red triangles are severe — you definitely want to avoid these if you can — but yellow and orange triangles are less so.

You can tap the Avoid Segment button to have Sprint Navigation plot an alternate route; if you do, Sprint Navigation displays an available alternative and asks you to accept it. When you tap Accept, your new route will be started — just follow the navigation instructions on the screen.

Tap the Minimize All Delays button to have Sprint Navigation plot a route that avoids all problem segments.

The little slider isn't really a slider but just an indication of average speed of the road segment.

Caution symbol

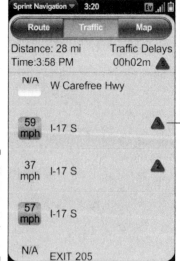
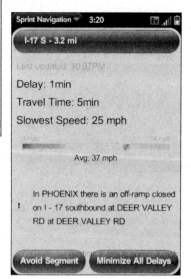

Figure 12-10:
Viewing
traffic
information
along your
route.

Searching for a contact's address

You can easily plot a route from your current location to any contact's address.

1. **Tap Drive To on the Sprint Navigation main screen and then tap Contact.**

   You see a list of contacts for whom you recorded addresses (see Figure 12-11).

2. **Tap the contact you want.**

   Sprint Navigation creates a route, a 3-D map appears (similar to the one shown earlier in Figure 12-5), and Sprint Navigation begins to give you verbal turn-by-turn directions to the address.

3. **Tap the address on the map to view written turn-by-turn directions, view an overview of the route, or check traffic along the route.**

Searching for nearby places

Here's one of my favorites: finding the cheapest gas.

1. **On the Sprint Navigation main screen, tap Search.**

2. **On the screen that appears, tap the Category box to see a list of categories for which you can search (see the left side of Figure 12-12).**

3. **Tap Gas by Price.**

   If you want, you can further refine your search by specifying a subcategory. For example, when you tap Gas by Price, you can then choose from Any, Regular, Plus 89, Premium, or Diesel.

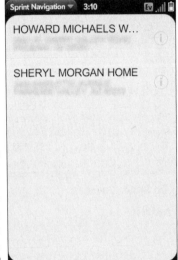

Figure 12-11: The contacts for whom you have set up addresses.

Figure 12-12: Selecting the category of the destination, and the results.

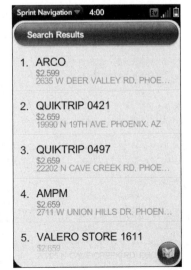

4. **Tap the Search button (hidden in the left side of Figure 12-12 behind the pop-up menu that appeared).**

   Sprint Navigation displays a list of gasoline stations near you, sorted in the order of least expensive to most expensive, as shown on the right side of Figure 12-12).

5. **Tap any gas station to view the screen shown earlier in Figure 12-3.**

6. **Tap the Drive To button to have Sprint Navigation plot a route and provide verbal and visual turn-by-turn directions.**

Other stuff you can do in Sprint Navigation

As I mention earlier in the chapter, you can save any destination to the Favorites folder, which is accessible from the Drive To and Share & More screens, whenever you see the screen shown in Figure 12-13. Just follow these steps:

1. **Search for a destination using the Search screen.**

2. **Tap an individual result of the search.**

3. **Tap the Save button.**

   Sprint Navigation drops the information in the Favorites folder.

4. **To view the saved destination and plot a route, tap Drive To on the main Sprint Navigation screen.**

5. **Then tap Favorites; and from the list that appears, tap the place you want to go.**

   Sprint Navigation plots a route and provides verbal and visual instructions.

You also can recall a set of directions from the Recent Places folder, available from the list that appears when you tap Drive To from the application's main screen.

Use the Map & Traffic option on the main Sprint Navigation menu to view your current GPS location and the traffic in that location.

Figure 12-13: From the destina- tion details screen, you can save a loca- tion to the Favorites folder.

When you tap Share & More on the main Sprint Navigation screen, you see a few items that you can tap:

- ✔ **Share Address:** Send an address as a text message to a contact, which is a convenient way to quickly let someone know where you are. By default, this will send your current address, but you can change it to send any location of your choosing.

- ✔ **Save Current Location:** Save your current location as a Favorite. You're given an opportunity to add a text label to the location before it's saved so that it's easier for you to identify in the future.

- ✔ **My Favorites:** Like going to the Drive To function from the main screen, another way to access your list of Favorites that you've saved.

- ✔ **Preferences:** Set preferences for Sprint Navigation, such as deciding between imperial and metric units, choosing whether the spoken voice played during navigation should pronounce street names, and more.

- ✔ **About:** Get support information (for technical troubles with the application and see your PIN (the a code required to log in to Sprint Navigation). You shouldn't have to know this code because Sprint Navigation remembers it for you.

Finding Your Way with Google Maps

Google Maps on your Pre doesn't provide live navigation. Instead, you can use Google Maps to find a specific business, a type of business, an address, or an intersection — and then get a route to the location from your present position. Google Maps can walk you through getting from your current location to your destination, but it doesn't talk to you nor does it track your progress; instead, it relies on you to step yourself through the directions. You can think of it like the world's best, easiest, and most complete fold-up paper map — and you'll never struggle to get it folded.

You can use the Google Maps app directly, or you can launch it from a variety of places on your Pre to get specific map information while performing some other task.

Using the Google Maps app

Follow these steps to have Google Maps plot your course:

1. **To load the Google Maps app, tap the Launcher icon on the main screen of your Pre.**

2. **Then, swipe from right to left in Launcher until you find the Google Maps app; then tap it.**

   Like Sprint Navigation, Google Maps uses Location Services (or Wi-Fi if you're outside the Sprint Network). When you open the app, Google Maps prompts you to allow Location Services to run (see the left side of Figure 12-14).

3. **Tap Allow.**

   Google Maps plots your current location and displays it on a map like the one shown on the right side of Figure 12-14.

On the map shown on the right side of Figure 12-14, your current position is represented by the small, flashing blue dot. You can slide the map around to view the area; the blue dot representing your current location does not have to appear onscreen. You can zoom in or out using the Pinch gesture (also discussed in Chapter 3):

✔ **To zoom out:** Place your thumb and forefinger together on the screen and slide them apart.

✔ **To zoom in:** Place your thumb and forefinger apart on the screen and slide them together.

Figure 12-14:
Google
Maps
prompts
you to use
Location
Services
and then
plots your
location.

Center Position button

Your location

If you can't see your position anymore, you can redisplay it by tapping the large blue-dot button that remains at the bottom of any screen displaying a map. The blue-dot button centers your current location on the map; I call it the Center Position button from this point forward.

From this map, you can begin searching. At the top of the screen, type the name of a business you want to find, or type a kind of business such as dry cleaners. If you already know the address of the place to which you want to go, you can type the address. Or, you can type an intersection.

If you opt to type an intersection, you'll have better luck with your searches if you also include a Zip code for the intersection (if you happen to know it offhand).

Type in the text box at the top of the screen and then press Enter. When you search, Google Maps produces results relative to your current location, displaying a map with results marked as balloons. If Google Maps returns more than one result, the balloon containing the black dot represents the selected search result (see the left side of Figure 12-15). You can tap any other balloon to select it and see information about it.

Search result

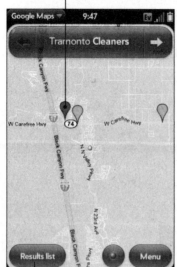

Figure 12-15:
The results
of a search
for dry
cleaners.

Click to see a list of nearby locations.

You can tap the Results List button to see a list of nearby locations, including their addresses, as shown in the right side of Figure 12-15. To get the phone number for a particular location, you can tap that entry. You also can get directions to that entry, see it on the map, or return to the list.

If you tap the phone number, Pre launches the Phone dial pad, ready for you to dial. You also can tap the Add to Contacts button at the bottom of the dialer, and the phone number appears in a contact card; you can fill in the name and address by switching between the Google Maps app and the Contacts app.

You don't need to dig that deep, though, if you can identify the location to which you want directions on the map.

1. **While viewing the map, tap the Menu button.**

   Google Maps displays the screen shown on the left side of Figure 12-16.

2. **Tap Get Directions.**

   Google Maps displays the screen shown in the right side of Figure 12-16, with your current location filled in as the starting location, and the destination location contains the address of the result selected on the map. You can change the starting location by simply typing in the box.

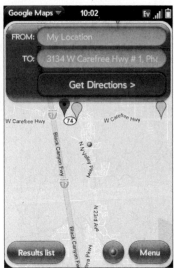

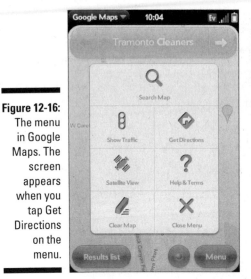

Figure 12-16:
The menu in Google Maps. The screen appears when you tap Get Directions on the menu.

Tap Get Directions at the top of the screen, and Google plots a route for you like the one shown in Figure 12-17. Your starting location is represented by a green balloon containing a dot, and your destination appears as a red balloon. Turns along the way appear as small blue dots.

Destination   Turns

Figure 12-17:
Google plots a route.

Start

You can keep the Map view onscreen as you follow the directions. Tap the right arrow at the top of the map to see the first direction, and continue tapping that arrow to see subsequent directions. As you move through each direction, Google Maps displays a blue dot on the route to mark your position in relation to the directions. In Figure 12-18, you see the map in Satellite view, and the current location marker matches a left turn at W. Westland Road shown at the top of the map. To view your map in Satellite view, tap the Menu button and then tap Satellite View.

Figure 12-18:
A satellite
view of a
Google Map
route.

Current location marker

Tap to see directions in list format.

If you don't want to view the map but prefer to see the directions in list format, tap the Directions List button in the bottom left of the Google Maps screen.

You can do a couple of other things while working in Google Maps:

✔ To see traffic conditions around your location and between your position and your destination, tap the Menu button and then tap Show Traffic. Repeat this process to remove traffic from view; the menu button will toggle to Hide Traffic.

✔ To start a new search, tap the Menu button and then tap Clear Map.

Mapping while you work

Google Maps is highly integrated with other apps on your Pre. Suppose that you need directions to get from your current location to the location of a contact. You don't need to launch the Google Maps app; instead, you can display the contact and tap one of the addresses you stored for the contact. Google Maps launches automatically and displays a map with the contact's address pinpointed. From there, you can tap the Menu button and then tap Get Directions to plot a route from your current location to your contact's location.

While working in Calendar, you can launch Google Maps directly for any event for which you've entered a location. Open an event that has a location specified, tap the Calendar application menu, and then tap Map Location. Google Maps launches, displaying a map pinpointing the location. You can then tap the Menu button in Google Maps and then tap Get Directions to plot a route from your current location to the event's location.

Some third-party apps available for the Pre also integrate with Google Maps. For example, while you use Flixster to search for a theater playing the movie you want to see (see Chapter 15 for more on how to do that), you can tap an icon associated with the theater's address to launch Google Maps and pinpoint the theater's location. Then, you can tap the Menu button in Google Maps and then tap Get Directions to plot a route from your current location to the theater.

Third-Party Navigation Options

In addition to the apps that come with your Pre, you'll find at least three location-based apps that you can download from the App Catalog to help you find stuff: Mobile by Citysearch, WHERE, and GoodFood.

Mobile by Citysearch

Mobile by Citysearch uses your location to help you find nearby banks, cafes, restaurants, or movie theaters. It then teams up with Google Maps to provide directions. You can submit recommendations about the places you find using Mobile by Citysearch; you also can share your present location with people in your address book using e-mail, SMS, or Twitter.

Like with other apps that use Location Services, this app prompts you to permit Location Services to run. After you allow Location Services, the first screen of Mobile by Citysearch shows featured businesses (see Figure 12-19). You can tap the tabs above the featured restaurant to see places to drink, shop, relax, and visit.

Figure 12-19:
Mobile by
Citysearch
initially
displays a
featured
restaurant.

You also can tap the Nearby tab above the featured listings to search for nearby businesses by category: Restaurant, Bars, Cafes, Banks, Movie Theaters, Shopping, Gas Stations, Clubs, Hotels, Salons & Spas, Arts & Entertainment, Attractions, Bakeries, and Pharmacies. After you drill into one of these categories, Mobile by Citysearch lists its findings; at the bottom of the screen, you can tap the left button to change the sort order from Distance to sort by rating or alphabetically.

When you drill down into any listing, Mobile by Citysearch gives the options of calling, showing the entry on a map — and uses Google Maps to display that map — write a review, share the location with a contact by e-mail, text, or tweet, bookmark the location, or visit its Web site. If you opt to call, tap the phone number, and the Pre's phone dialer launches and dials the number for you.

Mobile by Citysearch is new and doesn't have a large number of listings at this time, but that's sure to grow over time.

WHERE

After you allow Location Services to function when you launch WHERE, you find a pretty robust app that helps you easily search for a variety of common stuff as shown in Figure 12-20. You can do the following:

✔ Get up-to-date weather, using AccuWeather.

✔ Read your pick of local and national news.

✔ Get a traffic report for your location.

✔ Find a nearby business, like a Starbucks.

✔ Find gas prices organized by stations closest to you.

Figure 12-20: The main screen of WHERE.

WHERE includes access to the local review service Yelp, which you can use to read reviews about restaurants, shopping, food, beauty and spas, active life, nightlife, health and medical, local services, home services, hotels and travel, and arts and entertainment for many major cities. Figure 12-21 shows a typical entry in Yelp; you can tap the phone number to launch the Pre dial pad and dial the number. You can use the button on the left at the bottom of the screen to launch Google Maps and get directions, and you can tap the button on the right at the bottom of the screen to add the entry to your Contacts.

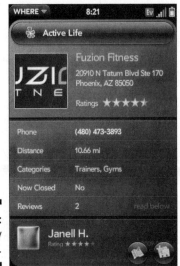

Figure 12-21:
A Yelp entry
in WHERE.

Using YP.com, you can search the Yellow Pages for restaurants, coffee shops, ATMs and banks, gas stations, hotels, airports, parking, movie theaters, and auto repair and towing services. A typical YP.com entry gives you the address and phone number; you can tap the phone number to launch the Pre dial pad and call the listing. You also can use the buttons at the bottom of an entry's screen to launch Google Maps and get directions or to add the entry to your Contacts.

When you tap the Movies button on WHERE, you see a list of movies playing, listed in alphabetical order; or, you can view movies by theater by tapping the Theaters button at the top of the screen. When you tap a movie entry, you get information and a synopsis of the movie; you can tap the button in the lower right of the screen to see what others on the WHERE Wall are saying about the movie (see Figure 12-22). Tap the Showtimes button to see a list of theaters showing the movie; just tap one to see its show times. You can use the buttons at the bottom of the screen to launch Google Maps to get directions to the theater, add the theater to your Contacts, and add an event to your Calendar to go see the movie.

GoodFood

When you want to focus on food near your location, try GoodFood to help you find nearby restaurants. The main screen of GoodFood, shown in Figure 12-23, displays a map of your location with small push pins representing restaurants nearby. You can use the pinch gesture to zoom in or out on the map. If you prefer to see a list of restaurants, tap the button in the upper right of the GoodFood screen.

The button in the upper left centers the map on your current location; if you tap this button, there's no way to get back to the original screen you saw when you opened the app except by closing and then re-opening GoodFood.

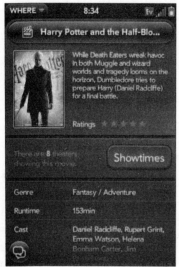

Figure 12-22: A movie entry in WHERE.

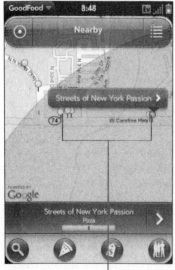

Figure 12-23: The main screen of GoodFood.

Tap a pushpin to see the restaurant name.

Tap any pushpin on the map to see the name of the restaurant; tap the name of the restaurant to see details about it (see Figure 12-24).

Figure 12-24:
A typical
entry in
GoodFood.

You can tap an arrow on an entry's screen to see a Google map and launch Google Maps to get directions, get more details about the entry, or read the reviews. To post your own review, you need to create an account with GoodFood and log into it; tap any button at the bottom of an entry's screen, and you'll be prompted to sign up.

You can use the buttons at the bottom of the main screen of GoodFood (refer to Figure 12-23) to search for a specific restaurant; filter displayed restaurants by type of food or price; or, if you signed up for a GoodFood account, leave a review of a restaurant.

Chapter 13

Rocking Out: Music on the Pre

*I*n this chapter, you discover everything you need to know to manage and listen to your favorite music right from the comfort of your Pre. It's easy, it works really well, and unless you have a massive collection of tracks that you want to be able to carry with you at all times, I'm willing to bet the Pre is the only portable music player you need.

How the Pre Rocks the House

Many phones have built-in music players, but very few phones play music *well.* Why is that? There are many good theories, but the way I see it, a phone (or any device, for that matter) needs a bare minimum of three basic things to do your favorite tracks justice:

✔ **Plenty of storage space:** It doesn't matter how great a phone sounds when you start blasting the tunes. If it can hold only a few of them, it doesn't do you any good. A phone needs several gigabytes of storage space, enough for at least a few hundred songs to keep things interesting on long walks, runs, and road trips.

✔ **A standard audio jack:** Loudspeakers are nice on occasion, but most often, you'll probably want to be listening to music over headphones. It's nice if you can plug those headphones into your phone without a special adapter.

✔ **Great battery life for playing music:** What good is a music player with a dead battery? It makes a decent paperweight, but that's about it. With the Pre, listening to music won't drain your battery much faster than merely having the phone on, and you can always continue to blast the tunes while your Pre is attached to a charger.

✔ **Good music management:** Because much of (if not all) the music you own is likely already on your computer, you need a good way to get it onto your phone. As you buy or rip new music on your computer, it should be easy to update your phone with that new music as well. I tell you how in just a bit.

The great news is that the Pre is one of the very few phones to meet all these requirements, and to top it off, the Pre's music player is easy to use. You can also buy new music wherever you happen to be, thanks to the Amazon MP3 application that comes bundled with the phone.

Loading Music onto the Pre

Out of the box, the Pre starts as a clean slate, so all that music-playing prowess built into your phone really isn't doing you a lot of good just yet. Don't worry, though — you can fix that right away by loading music already stored on your computer.

There are a couple ways to get the music moved over, both of which will involve connecting the Pre to the computer where your music is stored:

1. **Connect the USB cable that came with your Pre (or an approved replacement cable) between an available USB port on your computer and the concealed micro-USB port on the side of the phone.**

   As soon as you connect the cable at both ends, you're greeted with three buttons that appear at the bottom of the Pre screen (see Figure 13-1).

Figure 13-1:
The Pre after plugging it into a computer.

2. **If you want to use iTunes to manage music on your Pre, tap Media Sync. Otherwise, tap USB Drive.**

When you choose the Media Sync or USB Drive options, the Pre turns into your computer's "slave" until you disconnect it from your computer. That is to say, in the meantime, you can't use your Pre to make or receive calls, compose messages, or run applications. Before you enter either the Media Sync or USB Drive mode, you'll be warned (see Figure 13-2) and given an opportunity to back out by pressing Cancel.

Figure 13-2: Make sure you don't need to use your phone for now.

3. **Tap OK to confirm your selection, or Cancel to back out.**

4. **Proceed to the upcoming sections, "Media Sync: Using iTunes" or "USB Drive: Managing the music files yourself," depending on your choice in Step 2.**

Forgot your wall charger? No problem! Just tap the third button on this screen — Just Charge — to let your Pre charge its battery from the current supplied by your computer's USB port. (It will charge slower than plugging it into the wall, but at least it'll charge!) In other words, as long as you have a computer and your USB cable, you're never far away from pumping a little extra juice into your Pre battery.

Media Sync: Using iTunes

Even if you're not already using an iPod, you might use iTunes to manage all the music on your laptop or desktop computer simply because it gets the job done, it's easy to use, and features like Genius and Cover Flow make it entertaining. I can't say that I blame you — it works really well!

Although Apple doesn't officially support connecting any device other than an iPod or an iPhone to iTunes for transferring music, Palm has a creative workaround: The Pre simply pretends to be an iPod. iTunes can't tell the difference, so when you connect it, the software treats your phone the same way it would any Apple-branded media player.

iTunes compatibility on the Pre should be considered a bonus feature — not necessarily something that you rely on! Palm and Apple both state that neither can guarantee that iTunes will always work with the Pre in future versions of the program. I feel confident that both companies will try their best to make sure this compatibility remains viable, but it's something to be aware of. Fortunately, as a workaround, you can always switch to the USB Drive method of managing your music, as I explain in the next section.

As I mention in the preceding section, you tap the Media Sync button after you connect the Pre to your computer to start the synchronization process with iTunes. Then after confirming your selection by tapping OK, open iTunes on your computer.

Depending on how you have iTunes set up on your computer, iTunes might automatically open after you tap Media Sync. Don't worry. You haven't done anything wrong. You'll be able to use iTunes and synchronize normally.

iTunes will detect that you connected a new media player (see Figure 13-3). Leave the Automatically Sync Songs to My iPod check box selected unless you have a specific reason to uncheck it because this option will allow iTunes to make sure that your Pre is up to date with all the music in the playlists that you set it up to synch with. That is, you won't have to do anything on your own to make sure the files get transferred, which is just like the experience you'd have with an iPod. Then click Done in the Set Up Your iPod dialog box (in iTunes) to continue.

If you have more music than will fit in the available storage space on your Pre, that's not a problem — iTunes will ask you if you'd like it to create a special playlist of music that just contains enough tracks to fill up your free space. It'll even randomly select songs for you!

Your Pre shows up as a tiny iPod icon in the left sidebar of iTunes (in the Devices section, as shown in Figure 13-4). That tells you that that it's connected — and if you set it to automatically sync, it'll start synchronizing your music now by transferring it directly into the Pre's onboard memory.

If you want to select the music that goes on your Pre yourself rather than letting iTunes decide, here's how:

Figure 13-3:
iTunes
prompts
you to set
up your Pre
for media
synchroni-
zation.

The Palm Pre item

Figure 13-4:
The Pre
appears as
a device in
the iTunes
sidebar.

1. **In iTunes, click the Palm Pre in the sidebar on the left side.**

   The Palm Pre screen fills the right side of the window, where you set options for how you want iTunes to work with the device.

2. **Click the Music tab.**

3. **Make sure that the Sync Music check box is selected and that the Selected Playlists option is selected. Choose your iTunes playlists that you want to synchronize with the Pre; see an example in Figure 13-5.**

   From now on, only the music in the playlists that you select will be transferred to the Pre. If you update any selected playlist with new music, the new music will be transferred automatically the next time you connect.

Figure 13-5:
Choose
the iTunes
playlists
you want to
sync with
the Pre.

The Pre is capable of playing only non-DRM audio files from iTunes: that is, files that don't include copy protection. Most recent iTunes-purchased tracks are non-DRM files — sometimes called "iTunes Plus" — but older files that you purchased through iTunes and have not upgraded to the newer format might not play. The good news is that you can usually upgrade old iTunes songs with copy protection to iTunes Plus; see `http://support.apple.com/kb/HT1711` for details on how to do this.

To tell whether a song has copy protection in iTunes, right-click the song on a PC (or hold the Control key and clicking the song on a Mac), choose the Get Info menu item, and look for the phrase `Protected AAC Audio File` in the window that appears. If you see this displayed, the file has copy protection, and the Pre won't be able to play it.

USB Drive: Managing the music files yourself

If you don't use iTunes or you would rather not have iTunes make decisions about how to synchronize music with your Pre, you can manage the music files yourself — and it's actually quite easy. If you've moved files between two folders before, you'll take to this like a fish to water.

After you connect the Pre to your computer and place the Pre into USB Drive mode, your phone will appear on your computer just like any other hard drive. On a Mac, you'll find it on the Desktop; on a Windows PC, it'll be in your Computer or My Computer window. Open this "drive" in a new window, create a new folder in it for your music (if you haven't already), and drag your music files from your PC to this folder. The folder can be named anything you like. The next time you start the Music application on the Pre, it automatically searches its memory looking for any songs you added, cataloging anything it finds. It can play MP3, AAC, and AAC+ files, which very likely covers most of or all your current music collection.

And that's it! When you want to delete music, you can just reverse the process: Open the Pre's "drive" on your computer, go into the music folder you created, and delete the tracks you no longer want.

When you're done using USB Drive mode and want to disconnect the Pre from your computer, be sure to "eject" it first. On a Windows PC, right-click the Pre's drive in the Computer or My Computer window and choose Eject. On a Mac, you can simply drag the Pre's drive to your Trash.

Using the Music Application

To start playing music on the Pre, open its built-in Music application. Simply open Launcher and tap the Music icon. When the application loads, you're taken to the Music Library screen.

The Music Library screen

The Music Library screen is organized into a few distinct areas, as you can see in Figure 13-6.

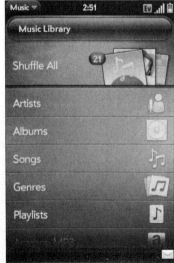

Figure 13-6:
The Music
Library
screen.

✔ **Current screen bar:** The gray bar at the top of the application tells you what screen you're seeing. If you were in the Artists screen instead of the Music Library screen, for example, it'd read Artists instead. When music is playing, a button labeled "Now Playing" appears on the right side of this bar that you tap to go to the Now Playing screen. (I discuss the Now Playing screen in the section, "Viewing the Now Playing screen" a little later on in the chapter.)

✔ **Shuffle All:** The first menu item simply shuffles your entire music collection — every single song you have on the Pre — and starts playing them as one long playlist. It's the quickest, easiest way to start playing music without having to drill down and choose a specific artist, genre, or playlist; it's also great for parties and for discovering music that you forgot you had! The graphic on the right depicts the album art for some of the songs in your collection, and the number to the left of the graphic gives you a count of the total number of songs that the Music application holds.

✔ **Artists:** Tap this menu item for an alphabetized list of all the artists whose songs you have.

✔ **Albums:** This menu item presents an alphabetized list of all the albums you have loaded.

✔ **Songs:** Want to impress yourself with the sheer number of tracks you've got at your disposal? Tap this menu item to display all your songs as one, long, sorted list.

✔ **Genres:** This is similar to the Albums menu item in behavior, but songs are sorted by their genre rather than by their album.

✔ **Playlists:** If you loaded music via iTunes and the Pre Media Sync mode, this menu item offers you access to any playlists that were synchronized by iTunes.

✔ **Amazon MP3:** This opens the Amazon MP3 store, where you can instantly preview and buy new tracks right from your Pre.

Next, take a look at how you'll actually get into your music and start listening to it. That's what it's there for, after all, right?

The Artists, Albums, Songs, Genres, and Playlists screens

Like with most music players, you can browse your collection of music in the usual ways: by artist, album, song name, genre, or playlist. All these screens work in essentially the same way, so simply for illustration, I show you an example using the Artists screen. To get there, simply tap the Artists menu item on the Music Library screen (refer to Figure 13-6).

From the Artists screen (see Figure 13-7), you have one-press access to every artist whose music is loaded on your Pre. It's sorted alphabetically with each letter's artists broken by a separator bar, making it easier to read. On the right is a sample of the artist's album art, and to the immediate left of that displayed in a bubble are the number of tracks you have for that particular artist.

First letter in artist's name

Number of tracks for artist

Separater bar   Album art

Searching

In any of these category screens — Artists, Albums, and so on — you can
search for exactly what you want rather than having to scroll through a
massive list to find it.

To search, just start typing a part of the item you're looking for (see
Figure 13-8). For example, if you're in the Artists screen and you're looking
for Aaron Copland, you could start typing **aar**, and all the artists without
"aar" in their names would immediately become hidden. Or say you want to
search for all the songs in an album that share a common letter.

As shown in Figure 13-8, I entered the letter "k" in the search area while
viewing one particular Aaron Copland album. Underneath the search area,
you can see the two songs from that album that contain the letter "k." (While
you won't be performing searches like this very often, you might search for
a song you know starts with a particular word or letter.) You'll see the term
you're searching for in a gray area near the top of the screen as you type with
a small magnifying glass to the left of it. To cancel your search and see all the
entries again, perform a back gesture (a quick swipe from right to left) on the
black gesture area below the screen (as discussed in Chapter 3).

Magnifying glass   Number of tracks

Enter a letter to search for

Figure 13-8:
Searching
for songs on
the Pre that
contain the
letter "k."

Search results

Track lists

When you tap the name of an artist, album, genre, or playlist, you are taken to a list of individual tracks (see Figure 13-9). Like the Music Library screen, you have the option to shuffle every track with a Shuffle All menu item at the top (which also shows the total number of tracks in the category toward the right side of the screen). The difference here is that you'll be shuffling only tracks within the category you selected — not your entire music library. This is helpful for shuffling all your Jimi Hendrix songs, the *Wicked* soundtrack, or the bluegrass music on your Pre.

Otherwise, you have access to every track in this category directly below the Shuffle All menu item — just press a song to play it. Selecting a specific song also loads the remainder of the songs from this category in the same order that you see them in the list here so that they're ready to play. This allows you to move between tracks just like you would on a CD. You can think of this as a temporary playlist.

If you want to play a whole album in correct order, select the album then press on the first track in the album's screen.

Figure 13-9:
A track
listing.

Viewing the Now Playing screen

Finally, you're getting to listen to some music! The Now Playing screen is your home base for music that is currently playing — hence the name — and it's available in two different views, depending on your style. See what I mean in Figure 13-10.

Album Art View button   List View button

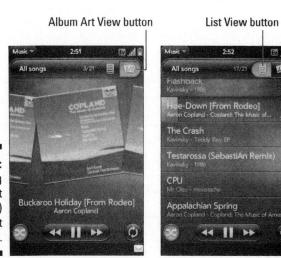

Figure 13-10:
Now Playing
in Album Art
view (left)
and List
view (right).

✔ **Album Art view:** If you work better with pictures than you do with words, Album Art view is probably for you. In this view, every track is represented by a large picture of its album art in the middle of the screen with track and artist names appearing at the bottom. You can move between tracks quickly by swiping your finger left and right on the album art.

✔ **List view:** List view *sounds* boring, but it's actually quite nice! Tracks in the current playlist appear in order, and each row includes the track name, artist, and album name. Additionally, the playing track appears highlighted and includes time elapsed and time remaining information on the right side of the row. While the track plays, the entire row progressively fills up with a blue bar to give you a visual estimate of how much song you have remaining.

To switch between Album Art and List views, just touch the buttons at the right side of the screen bar that's at the top of the application.

By holding your finger down on a track while in List view, you can rearrange the order it'll play in — just like rearranging cards or icons. (Read more about cards and rearranging them in Chapter 3.)

At the bottom of either view, you have the usual playback controls in the middle — Previous Track, Play/Pause, and Next Track. At the left is a Shuffle button that turns blue when enabled; when on, the tracks in your current playlist are reordered. You can return to the original track order by pressing the Shuffle button again.

At the right side of the bottom, the Repeat button allows you to repeat the current playlist (by pressing once so that it's blue) or just the current song (by pressing a second time).

Keeping the music going

When you press Play, that doesn't mean you need to stay in the Music application until you're done listening to tunes. In fact, you're free to move around to e-mail, the Web application, or any other app on the Pre — just return to Card View by pressing the Center button in the gesture area below the screen and select another card, go to Launcher, or perform any other action you like. (See Chapter 3 for more details on moving between applications.)

As you leave the Music application, a notification at the bottom of the screen (shaped like a musical note) reminds you that you still have music playing. By pressing on the notification, you'll be able to see what's playing, move between tracks, pause, and restart the music.

Chapter 14

Relaxing with Your Pre

***W**hen it's time to relax, your Pre is your friend. In addition to all the things your Pre can do to help you organize your life and stay connected via phone or text messaging, entertainment is never far away. You can listen to the radio, watch TV and movies, play a few games, and even follow NASCAR racing on your Pre — read on!

You also can browse the Web, shoot photos and videos, and play music on your Pre; see Chapters 10, 11, and 13 for details.

Listening to the Radio

Using your Pre, you can listen to a wide variety of radio stations — and if none of them suits you, you can download an app that you can customize to play the type of music you want to hear.

Using Sprint Radio

Sprint Radio, an app that comes with your Pre, gives you access to hundreds of radio stations located across the country. Even if you live in Colorado, you can listen to radio stations from New York City. Many radio stations available via your Pre are free, and you'll also find subscription channels available. In addition to radio stations, you'll find some bonus material such as music videos, interviews, and live concerts.

You use the Sprint TV (yes, I said Sprint TV) app to access these radio stations; just follow these steps:

1. **Tap the Launcher icon on the main screen.**

2. **Swipe from right to left in Launcher until you find the Sprint TV app; tap that.**

   The Pre displays the main screen of the Sprint TV app (see Figure 14-1).

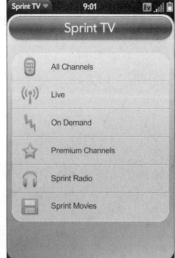

Figure 14-1: The main screen of the Sprint TV app.

3. **Tap Sprint Radio to see the list of radio station categories available (see Figure 14-2).**

Categories displayed in yellow represent subscription radio stations for which you pay a fee, whereas free content appears in gray. Feel free to tap a subscription category; you won't be charged anything until you opt to sign up.

Tap a radio station category to see the stations available in that category:

- ✓ **Sprint Radio:** Ten commercial-free radio stations that stream a variety of different types of music to your Pre.

- ✓ **SEE (Sprint Exclusive Entertainment) Music:** Music videos as well as live streaming radio stations that play Hip-Hop, Rock, Pop, and Latin music. You'll also find music news and interviews.

- ✓ **Sprint Radio Premier:** Bonus offerings (like seasonal stations for different times of the year), Sprint Radio's Top 10 Countdown Show, and a wide variety radio stations presented by genre and by region (see Figure 14-3).

Gray indicates free content.

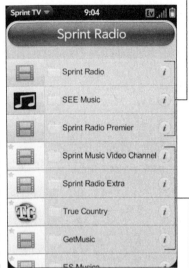

Figure 14-2:
Display
Sprint Radio
to see a list
of radio
station
categories.

Yellow indicates subscription based content.

✔ **Sprint Music Video Channel:** Are you a music video junkie? Did you grow up sitting in front of MTV and VH1 for hours on end? If so, check out the Sprint Music Video Channel subscription service for the hottest videos out there.

✔ **Sprint Radio Extra:** If the ten channels provided in Sprint Radio aren't enough for you, Radio Extra — which costs $5.95 per month — gives you another 50 channels to check out.

Suppose, for example, that you want to listen want to listen to live streaming radio from WFUS in the Tampa Bay area of Florida. In Sprint Radio Premier, tap Local Radio by Region to display the available regions (shown on the left side of Figure 14-4). Then, if you tap Florida, you see a list of Florida-based stations that stream radio content over the Web (shown on the right side of Figure 14-4).

When you select a station, your Pre connects to the Internet and begins playing the radio station's content. Onscreen, your Pre automatically switches to landscape mode and displays the radio's logo along with the song title and the artist performing the song.

Use the Volume buttons on the left side of the Pre to raise or lower volume.

Figure 14-3:
Sprint Radio
Premier
offers
bonuses as
well as live
streaming
radio by
genre and
by region.

Figure 14-4:
Finding
regional
radio
stations.

Pandora

Want to create your own radio station? You know, one that plays the kind of music you like. For example, you might want '50s or '60s Rock, or classical music, neither of which is easily available via Sprint Radio. Use Pandora — available for download from the App Catalog — to create free streaming radio stations that play the types of music you want. Even better, it doesn't just play the music you tell it to — it actually takes examples of songs and artists you like and automatically creates stations that play similar music. As the music plays, you can rate individual songs, which helps Pandora refine the station for you so it only plays the stuff you love.

For details on downloading an app using the App Catalog, see Chapter 15.

Pandora is a Web-based service, and you can use it to listen to music from your desktop computer. If you are new to Pandora, you can set it up on your Pre. If you already use Pandora on the Internet, simply download the app to your Pre and log in.

Pandora on the Pre is fully integrated with your account on the Web, and any radio stations you created using your browser will appear on your Pre.

To set up Pandora on your Pre, follow these steps:

1. **Tap the Launcher icon on the main screen.**

2. **Swipe from right to left in Launcher until you find the Pandora app; tap that.**

   The Pre displays the screen shown in Figure 14-5.

Figure 14-5:
Setting up
Pandora to
use on
your Pre.

3. **Tap the I Am New To Pandora button to display the Create a Free Account screen shown in Figure 14-6.**

4. **Supply an e-mail address, a password (minimum of five characters), your birth year, and your Zip code; then tap the Male button or the Female button.**

Figure 14-6:
Complete
the sign-up
screen for
Pandora.

5. **(Optional) Scroll down the screen to opt to receive personalized recommendations and tips.**

6. **Read the Privacy Policy and Terms of Agreement, and select the check box that indicates that you agree with both.**

7. **Tap the Sign Up button.**

   Read the following section to see how to add your first radio station.

Adding a radio station

The first time you sign in to Pandora, you set up a radio station. If you've used Pandora on the Internet, the radio stations you created there appear on your Pre.

If you're using Pandora for the first time, after you complete the sign-up screens shown in the preceding section, use the next screen that appears to type the name of an artist or composer whose music you like, or the name of a song you like. As you type, Pandora begins displaying possible matches (shown on the left in Figure 14-7).

When you make a selection from the list, Pandora creates a radio station for you (shown on the right in Figure 14-7) and starts playing music that is similar in style to your selected type.

List button

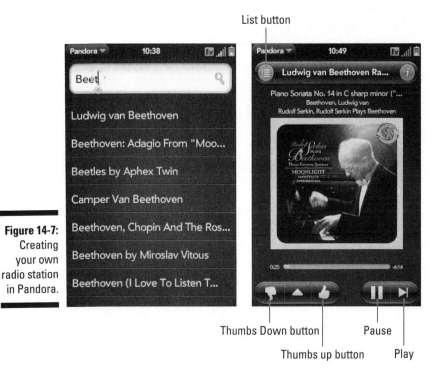

Figure 14-7:
Creating
your own
radio station
in Pandora.

Thumbs Down button | Pause

Thumbs up button | Play

To pause the song that's playing, tap the Pause button in the lower-right corner; tap the Play button beside the Pause button to resume listening.

You can rate the song you hear by tapping the Thumbs Up button or the Thumbs Down button in the lower-left corner of the screen. Tap the button between the Thumbs Up button and the Thumbs Down button to bookmark the current song or the artist, buy the album, or tell Pandora to not repeat the song for one month.

To view the list of radio stations you created (see Figure 14-8), tap the List button in the upper left of the Pandora screen, just below the Pandora menu in the Now Playing screen. With the exception of the first time you log in to Pandora, you'll see this screen each time you log in to Pandora.

A small megaphone appears to the right of the radio station you're listening to. While viewing the list of radio stations you created, you can create another radio station; tap the Plus sign button in the lower-left corner. Pandora displays the screen you see in Figure 14-9. (More about that QuickMix button in a bit.)

QuickMix

Figure 14-8:
The list of radio stations you created.

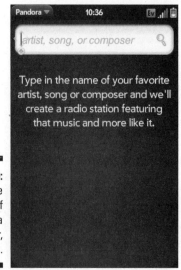

Figure 14-9:
Type the name of an artist, a composer, or a song.

Type the name of an artist, a composer, or a song you like. Pandora searches for likely matches and displays the screen shown earlier on the left side of Figure 14-7. Make a selection, and Pandora creates the station for you.

Pandora things you can do on the Web

Whether you had a Pandora account before you got your Pre, or you created your Pandora account from your Pre, your account is a Web-based account, and you can view your account from your browser on your computer and make changes to it. In fact, you can make certain changes only from your computer's browser.

For example, you might be wondering about the QuickMix button that appears at the top of your list of radio stations (refer to Figure 14-8). Tapping the QuickMix button essentially shuffles all radio stations you include in the QuickMix so that you can play a rotation of stations. You can create a QuickMix using your browser. After that, just tap the QuickMix button on your Palm Pre to play the rotation.

To work with your account on your computer, open your browser and go to Pandora online (www.pandora.com). Click the Sign In link near the top of the page and enter your sign-in information to display your information (see Figure 14-10).

Figure 14-10:
Pandora on
the Web.

Your list of radio stations appears on the left. To create a QuickMix

1. **Click QuickMix at the bottom of your list.**

2. **When Pandora displays a box that lists your stations, place checks beside the ones you want to include in the QuickMix.**

You can include all your stations in the QuickMix, but you can create only one QuickMix at a time.

To change what you include in your QuickMix

1. **In Pandora, click the down arrow beside the QuickMix button to display a menu of choices.**

2. **Choose Edit QuickMix Details from that menu and change your selections.**

From your browser, you can also expand the content for a particular radio station. Click the down arrow beside the station's name (see Figure 14-11) and choose Add Variety to This Station. Pandora displays a box where you can type the name of an artist, a composer, or a song. When you click the Add button, Pandora adds similar content to your radio station. The new content is also available on your Pre.

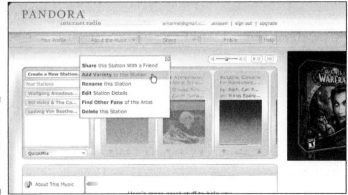

Figure 14-11:
Opening
a station's
menu in
Pandora.

Finally, you can rename a radio station. Again, click the down arrow beside the station's name; from the menu that appears, choose Rename This Station. Pandora displays a box where you can type a new name for the station. The new name appears on your Pre both in List view and when you play the station.

It might take a few minutes for the updates from your browser to reach your Pre.

TV Goes Mobile

Using the Sprint TV app, you can watch live television on your Pre. Many channels available to you are free — and, if you're interested, you can subscribe to the Premium offerings.

The first time you try to view a channel that requires a subscription, you'll see a prompt that asks you to purchase access to the channel. So, there's no need to worry about hidden charges.

To view live television on your Pre, follow these steps:

1. **Tap the Launcher icon on the main screen.**

2. **Swipe from right to left in Launcher until you find the Sprint TV app; tap that.**

   Pre displays the main screen of the Sprint TV app (see Figure 14-12).

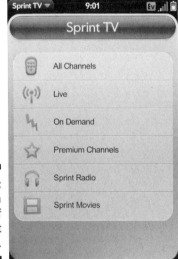

Figure 14-12: The main screen of the Sprint TV app.

3. **Make your choice:**

   - *All Channels:* View all available TV channels.
   - *Live:* See live TV offerings.
   - *On Demand:* See offerings that are, well, on demand.
   - *Premium Channels:* Choose from exclusively subscription content that you'll need to purchase.

Live and On Demand contain both free content and subscription content. You can easily identify the subscription content because the options appear in yellow, whereas free content appears in gray. (Read more about choosing On Demand in a bit.)

For this example, tap Live, and a screen similar to the one shown in Figure 14-13 appears.

4. **Tap a program.**

It loads onto your Pre. Most programs view in landscape mode, so rotate your Pre so that the keyboard is located on the right side of the Pre.

Figure 14-13: In Sprint TV, see programs available for live viewing.

To stop playback of a Sprint TV station, just perform a back gesture on the black Gesture bar below the screen. (See Chapter 3 for a refresher on gestures.) You'll be taken back to the program guide.

When you tap On Demand on the screen shown in Figure 14-12, you see offerings similar to the ones shown in Figure 14-14; the available offering update as your Pre synchronizes with the Palm servers. When you tap a choice from the On Demand menu, your Pre displays available content in that choice. For example, if you tap USA, you can watch video clips from a variety of shows that run on the USA Network, such as *Monk*, *Psych*, *Burn Notice*, and *Law and Order CI*. You also can view full episodes for USA Network TV shows, based on availability. You'll find similar types of content on the other channels.

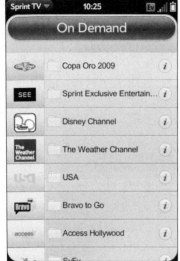

Figure 14-14:
Offerings
available
through On
Demand.

Popcorn, Anyone?

In addition to watching TV, you have a couple of ways to watch movies on your Pre. You can use Sprint TV, or you can download Flixster and Fandango from the App Catalog. You pay for each movie as you select it.

You can watch videos from YouTube using either the Web browser or the YouTube app on your Pre; for details on using the YouTube app, see Chapter 11.

Using Sprint Movies

One of the categories available on the opening menu of the Sprint TV app is Sprint Movies (refer to Figure 14-12). When you tap Sprint Movies, you see the screen shown in Figure 14-15, which organizes movie offerings into categories. You'll pay $4.99 and up depending on the movie to watch the content available in the Now Playing category, but you can tap into the category to view the offerings — and, in many cases, you can view a free preview of the offerings. You can view the offerings in alphabetical order or by genre: action, comedy, drama, and horror. You also can view new releases as well as the content in the What's Hot category.

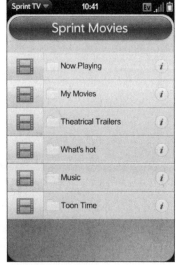

Figure 14-15:
Content
available
through
Sprint
Movies.

The content you find in the Theatrical Trailers category is free to view.

Using Flixster

You can use Flixster to plan a visit to the movie theater or DVD rental store. You can search for movies by title, director, or actor. Read reviews and watch trailers for movies about to be released as well as movies already in the theaters and movies on DVD. For movies playing in the theaters, you can get theater information with maps, phone numbers, show times; and you can buy tickets online through MovieTickets.com.

You can't use Flixster to find a DVD rental store, but you can still use the Pre's navigation capabilities to do that — see Chapter 12 for details.

Flixster, a free app as of the writing of this book, is available through the App Catalog; see Chapter 15 for details on downloading an app from the App Catalog. Flixster uses Location Services on your Pre to display movie information pertinent to your geographic location; you'll be prompted to allow Location Services to run when you install Flixster.

When you first load Flixster, you see movies about to be released (see Figure 14-16).

Figure 14-16:
When you
first open
Flixster,
you see
movies that
will open in
the current
week.

The movies are organized by popularity, but you can tap the button in the upper right to view movies sorted by ratings or by title.

When you scroll down the screen, you see movies playing in the theaters, organized by Top Box Office movies and followed by those Also In Theaters. Tap a movie to view the Movie Info screen, which contains, well, information about the movie. From the Movie Info screen (shown on the left side of Figure 14-17), you can play the trailer; when you scroll down, you find critic reviews and ratings from Flixster and movie ratings Web site Rotten Tomatoes. If you tap either of the review percentages from Flixster or Rotten Tomatoes, the Pre Web browser launches and takes to you the site where you can read the details behind the percentage rating.

When you tap the Showtimes button, Flixster changes the appearance of the Movie Info screen to list the theaters near you that are playing the movie, along with the times the movie is playing (shown on the right side of Figure 14-17).

If you tap a particular theater in the list, the Ticket Info screen appears, displaying today's show times (see Figure 14-18); if you want to buy tickets for a different day, go back to the Movie Info screen and change the Date. On the Ticket Info screen, scroll to find the movie time in which you're interested; you can then tap the Calendar button beside the movie time and the Pre will prompt you to add the movie to your calendar.

Showtimes button

Figure 14-17:
Read a
movie
synopsis,
watch a
trailer, and
find show
times.

Movie info

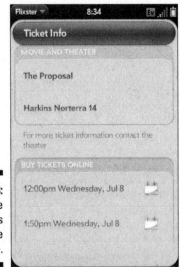

Figure 14-18:
Find movie
show times
for the
movie.

While viewing the Ticket Info screen, tap a movie time to have Flixster launch
MovieTickets.com, where you can proceed to purchase a ticket.

On the main screen of Flixster (refer to Figure 14-16), you can use the icons at the bottom of the screen to change the way you search for movies. Tapping the second icon from the left — the one that looks like a movie ticket — displays the Theaters screen, which, by default, shows theaters near you. When you tap any theater, you see the Theater Info screen. And, although the default view displays theaters near you, you can tap the button in the upper right corner of the Theaters screen to display theaters by name.

When you tap the middle button at the bottom of main Flixster screen, you can see movies that will be released in the future; the movies appear in date order, starting with those due to be released in the near future. You can tap a movie to read a synopsis and view the trailer.

When you tap the fourth button from the left— the one that looks like a DVD — Flixster displays the On DVD screen, where you can scroll through the approximately 50,000 movies available on DVD to view information about them and their trailers as well as read reviews.

Tapping the first button on the right (with the picture of the magnifying glass on it) enables you to search for movies by title, actor, or director.

Using Fandango

Fandango is another app that helps you plan a movie-going experience. Available from the App Catalog, Fandango uses Location Services on your Pre to help you get movie information; watch trailers; find movies in theaters near you; and, if online ticketing is available, buy tickets using your Fandango account or credit card information that you store in the Fandango Settings screen.

When you first launch Fandango, after accepting Location Services, you see a list of movies currently in theaters. The movies opening during the current week appear at the top of the list, followed by the top ten movies; and finally, you see a list of the rest of the movies playing currently (see Figure 14-19).

View information for movies not yet in theaters by tapping the Coming Soon button in the lower right of the main Fandango screen.

When you tap a movie, you see a synopsis of the movie (see Figure 14-20). Using the buttons at the bottom of this screen, you can watch the movie's trailer, read fan reviews of the movie, or view still photos from the movie.

If you scroll down the screen shown in Figure 14-20, you find a list of theaters near you at which the movie is playing (see Figure 14-21).

Figure 14-19: The main Fandango screen.

Figure 14-20: When you tap a movie, a synopsis appears.

When the Buy button appears beside a theater name, you can buy tickets online for the movie. Tap the Buy button to choose a time, and Fandango displays a screen like the one shown in Figure 14-22, where you can specify the number of tickets you want to buy and check out. To check out, enter credit card information that you have the option to store in your Fandango profile on the Pre, or you can sign in to your Web-based Fandango account.

Figure 14-21:
Below a movie's synopsis, you'll find a list of theaters and times that the movie is playing.

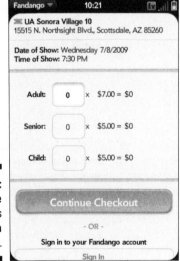

Figure 14-22:
Buy movie tickets online via Fandango.

After you purchase your ticket, Fandango gives you the option of saving an event for your movie on the Pre calendar.

If you prefer to plan your movie-going experience based on what's playing at a selected theater, tap the Theaters button at the top of main Fandango screen (refer to Figure 14-19). By default, Fandango sorts the theaters based on their proximity to your location, but you can tap the A–Z button to sort the theaters in your general area in alphabetical order.

The Fandango app lets you store some preference-type information to make your movie ticket purchase experience easier. Tap the Fandango menu and then tap Preferences & Accounts to view the screen shown in Figure 14-23.

Figure 14-23:
Store pref-
erences for
Fandango.

Among other options, you can change your Zip code, turn off Location Services, and store credit card information for Fandango to fill in if you decide to purchase tickets using a credit card.

As Fandango will indicate, your credit card information is secure. However, if you lose your Pre, you effectively also lose your credit card because it can then be used by anyone who finds your Pre. Also understand that when you buy tickets using a credit card, you can simply enter your credit card information at the time of purchase, and you don't need to store the information in you Pre.

Games and Your Pre

As of the writing of this book, not a lot of games are available yet for the Pre. But, over time, I'm sure that more games will become available. Keep an eye on the App Catalog, and also check the Palm Web site for games for the Pre:

```
www.palm.com/us/search/index.html?search=pre games
```

Too, many online game-hosting sites (think PopCap and the like) are starting to offer their games in a format that you can play on the Pre.

You can at least find a demo for Connect 4 as well as full versions of Speed Brain and Sudoko in the App Catalog.

Following NASCAR Racing

With the NASCAR Sprint Cup Mobile app on your Pre, you can keep up with NASCAR racing anytime you want. Using this app, you can view driver statistics and race results, and also listen to live race audio tracks. Initially, you set up a single driver whose activities you want to monitor, but after you're in the app, you can set up four other drivers to also monitor.

Tap the Launcher icon on the main screen of your Pre. Then, swipe from right to left in Launcher until you find the NASCAR app; tap that. The first time you open the NASCAR app, choose a driver by tapping a driver thumbnail. Then, the Home screen of the NASCAR app appears (see Figure 14-24). You can return to this screen any time by tapping the Home button at the bottom of the screen.

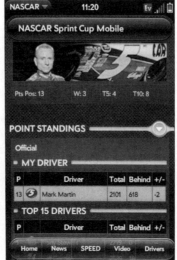

Figure 14-24: The main screen of the NASCAR app.

On the Home screen, you see the point standings for the driver you selected as your driver, along with the point standings of the top 15 drivers; scroll down the Home screen to see the point standings. At the bottom of the Home screen is the View More button, which you tap to see the point standings for all the drivers.

Tap the News button at the top of the NASCAR app to find news headlines about your driver, Sprint Cup standings, nationwide news, truck news, editorial news, photos, and lap-by-lap news. Categories are separated by a gold bar; when you tap the bar, Pre opens that category to show you its content (see Figure 14-25).

Figure 14-25: Wander among the various news categories.

Tap any item in a news category to view the whole news item.

Tap the SPEED button at the bottom of the NASCAR app screen to view NASCAR-associated video clips available on SPEEDtv.com. On this screen, you'll find the following categories separated by gold bars: NASCAR on SPEED, This Week in NASCAR, NASCAR Victory Lane, and NASCAR Performance. Just tap an item in a category to view the video.

Tap the Video button at the bottom of the NASCAR app screen to view videos from the following categories (again, separated by gold bars): Race Rewind, FedEx Preview, Beyond Pit Road, Final Laps, Sights, and Sounds, NASCAR Minute, Garage Pass, and NASCAR Today.

Tap Drivers to view the profile of the driver you initially selected when you first opened the NASCAR app. As shown in Figure 14-26, you also can view news stories concerning your selected drivers. And, using the last category on this screen, you can change your primary driver or add up to five secondary drivers whose progress you want to monitor.

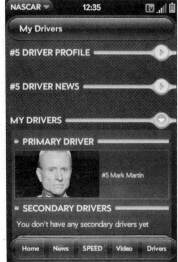

Figure 14-26:
View information specific to the drivers you're monitoring.

At the bottom of the screen is the Change My Drivers button (not visible in Figure 14-26). Tap that button, and the screen shown in Figure 14-27 appears. Tap the right side of any slot — including the first one that contains the driver you picked the first time you launched the NASCAR app — to see a list of drivers whose progress you can follow. Just tap the driver you want to add.

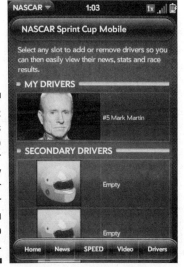

Figure 14-27:
Use this screen to change your primary driver or add other drivers you want to follow.

In addition to the buttons across the bottom of the NASCAR app screen, you can tap the choices available on the NASCAR app menu in the upper left of the screen. When you tap Stats and Schedules, the NASCAR app presents a screen that provides these categories: Sprint Race Recap, Latest NNS Results, Point Standings (also available on the Home screen), Season Statistics, and Season Schedule. Again, the categories are separated by a gold bar that you tap to see the items in the category.

When you tap Sprint FanZone on the NASCAR app menu, you get the opportunity to enter sweepstakes to win a variety of prizes associated with the NASCAR Sprint All-Star Race.

When you tap Alerts and Personalization on the NASCAR app menu, you can set up alerts to on a wide variety of subjects related to the race, including all NASCAR news, Sprint Cup news, flag status changes, and news that pertains to your selected driver, just to name a few. You also can view today's alerts, adjust your race-day audio settings, and customize your race weekend Home screen to display Leaderboard or Pit Pass information instead of the point standing information that appears by default.

Finally, when you tap Fantasy on the NASCAR app menu, the Fantasy screen appears (see Figure 14-28).

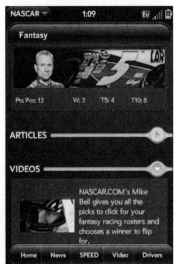

Figure 14-28:
The Fantasy
screen.

From this screen, you can view articles and videos associated with the Fantasy Cup Challenge game.

Chapter 15

Managing Your Apps

· ·

· ·

You probably wouldn't have a Pre if you weren't an "organizational" type. And, along with organizing yourself goes keeping your Pre in order and up to date. This chapter covers basic data management tasks, including adding/deleting apps and other stuff to your Pre, updating the Pre's webOS operating system, and backing up and restoring.

Downloading and Installing New Apps

You use the App Catalog to add applications to the Pre. The process is very easy. Because the Pre is so new, there aren't thousands of apps available yet. But, as time goes by, more and more apps will become available, and you'll no doubt want to try them out. (Have a peek at Chapter 16, by the way, for some of my favorites.)

At the time this book was written, the App Catalog was still considered a beta product: that is, a product being tested. You might notice the Beta banner that appears in the screenshots of the App Catalog as you read this section.

Before you install apps, I recommend checking the amount of space available on your Pre. Tap the Launcher button to display all the apps loaded on your Pre. Swipe from right to left in Launcher until you find Device Info. Tap it and look at the Available field under Phone (see Figure 15-1).

Your Pre has about 8 gigabytes of space that can be used by applications you install, pictures you take, music files you load, and anything else you happen to store (like attachments saved from e-mails). It's up to you how you decide to divvy up that space, but remember that installing more applications means that you'll have less space available for everything else.

How much space you have left

Figure 15-1:
Check available space on your Pre before you install an app.

Here are some ways to find an app you want to install:

- ✔ If you know the name of the app, search for it by name.
- ✔ Select the app from those listed as Featured or Popular.
- ✔ Search for apps by category, such as Entertainment or Utilities.

To find and install an app that you're interested in, follow these steps:

1. **Tap the Launcher button in the lower-right corner of the main screen.**

2. **Swipe from right to left in Launcher until you find the App Catalog; tap that.**

   The Pre displays the main screen of the App Catalog (see Figure 15-2).

   You might experience a short delay while the Palm Pre updates the entries available in the App Catalog.

3. **If you know the name of the app, type it in the Search field at the top of the screen.**

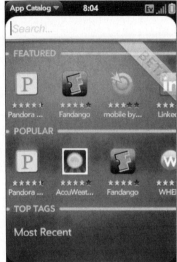

Figure 15-2:
The main
screen of
the App
Catalog.

4. **Press Enter on the keyboard or tap the Search icon that appears to the right of your search text.**

   You can also swipe to the right or left in the rows for Featured apps or Popular apps to view them. Otherwise, drag to scroll down in the App Catalog, where you'll see the categories by which you can review apps (see Figure 15-3).

Figure 15-3:
When you
drag down
in the App
Catalog, you
find catego-
ries of apps.

4. **Tap a category.**

   When it opens, you can view the apps in it (see Figure 15-4).

5. **Tap the app you're considering.**

   Information about the selected app appears onscreen. Typically, you'll find a few sample images of the application in action that you can tap to enlarge, the number of downloads for the app, and the number of reviews and the average rating (see Figure 15-5).

Figure 15-4: Apps available in a category selected on the App Catalog's home screen.

Figure 15-5: Initially, you see sample images from the app.

If you drag down, you'll find a description of the app (see Figure 15-6) and you can tap Reviews to read the reviews submitted for an app.

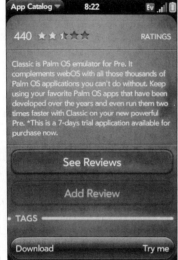

Figure 15-6: The App Catalog provides a description of the app.

If you drag down further, you see the categories that contain tags for the app (see Figure 15-7); you can tap a category to see other apps in that category. You also see links to the developer home page and application support; if you tap either link, you connect to the Internet via the Pre browser to land on the developer's site.

If you tap to view a category, use the Back gesture (see Chapter 3 or the Cheat Sheet for a refresher on gestures) to return to the information about the app.

6. **If you decide to install the app, tap the Download button at the bottom of the screen.**

Pre downloads a free application — or, in the case of an application that costs money, a trial of the application.

If you're downloading a trial version of a paid application, the terms of the trial will vary from app to app; some might limit which features are available before you pay, and others might work only for a limited period of time (say, seven days).

Check the developer's Web site before you download to determine whether a fee is associated with the app.

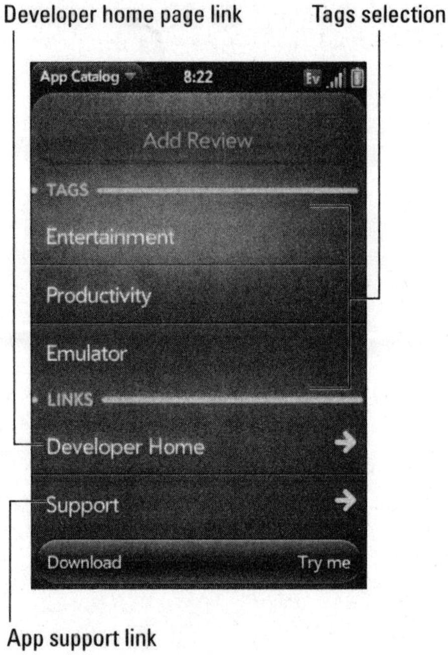

Developer home page link   Tags selection

Figure 15-7:
Tap a
category
in the Tags
section or,
below that,
one of the
links associ-
ated with
the app.

App support link

Adding Stuff from Your Computer to Your Pre

You can add pictures, music, and document files from your desktop to your Pre. For example, suppose that you want to use your dog's photo as your Pre wallpaper. Just upload the photo and then select it as the wallpaper. (Keep reading to see how.)

Or suppose that you have some PDF files on your computer that you want to transfer to your Pre. Just upload them and then use Pre's preinstalled PDF View app to open and view the PDF file.

You might be wondering how managing your files on your Pre like this differs from the synching discussed in other parts of this book, particularly when talking about your contacts, calendar, and other personal data. Put simply, when data is synched, your Pre automatically decides what to add, change, and remove based on what has been most recently added. By contrast, when you add files to your Pre, you're simply transferring files, just as you would move files between disk drives on your computer. There's no powerful computer brain trying to decide what files to copy for you here!

While your Pre is connected to your computer, you won't be able to make or receive calls or use any other Pre features.

To upload files from your computer to your Pre, follow these steps:

1. **Using the cable that came with your Pre, plug the USB end into your computer and the micro-USB end into your Pre.**

   Make sure your Pre is on when you perform this step. You'll probably hear a sound from your computer indicating that a new hardware device has been plugged in.

   If this is the first time you plugged in your Pre to your computer, let your computer go through the process of recognizing and setting up your Pre as a new piece of connected hardware that it can communicate with. You'll see a series of notification balloons in the system tray area. But, if the New Hardware wizard starts, simply close it.

2. **On your Pre, tap USB Device.**

   Your computer sets up your Palm Pre as a USB drive with its own drive letter; you can open this drive from your computer to view a list of folders just as you would any other hard drive or USB drive.

3. **Transfer the files you want.**

   - *To add photos:* Say you want to upload photos to use as wallpaper on your Pre. Just drag and drop the photos from your computer into the Wallpapers folder on the Pre USB drive.

     Photos can actually be stored anywhere on the Pre, and it will automatically detect them. I explain this concept in more detail in Chapter 11.

   - *To add PDF files that you can view with the Pre's PDF View app:* Drag and drop the PDF files from your computer into the Downloads folder on the Pre USB drive.

4. **When you're finished copying files from your computer to your Pre, you'll need to prepare it to be disconnected.**

   - *On a Windows computer:* Right-click the Safely Remove Hardware icon that appears in the system tray area in the lower-right corner of your computer screen and then choose Safely Remove Hardware.

   - *On a Mac:* Drag the Pre's drive icon from the Desktop to the Trash.

5. **When prompted, select the USB Mass Storage Device that represents your Palm Pre and then click the Stop button.**

   A second box appears.

6. **Select Palm Pre USB Device and then click OK.**

Setting wallpaper

You can use any picture in the Wallpapers folder as the background that appears on the main screen of your Palm Pre. Follow these steps:

1. **Tap the Launcher button.**

2. **Swipe from right to left in Launcher until you find the Photos app; then tap Photos.**

3. **Tap Wallpapers.**

4. **Tap the image you want to use to display it.**

5. **Tap the Wallpapers menu at the top of the screen.**

6. **From the menu that appears, tap Set Wallpaper.**

---

7. **Disconnect the cable connecting your Palm Pre to your computer.**

You can return to using all the Pre's features.

Out of the box, your Pre supports the types of files shown in Table 15-1 that can be opened using its built-in applications (but your Pre might support other files, depending upon the applications you've downloaded to it).

Table 15-1	Supported File Types
File Type	*Extensions*
Pictures	GIF, JPG, PNG, BMP
Videos	MPG, M4V, 3GP, 3G2
Music	MP3, M4A, WAV, AMR, AAC
Documents	PDF, DOC, DOCX, XLS, XLSX, PPT, PPTX

Working with Installed Apps

With so many apps available on your Pre, a little app management is in order. Occasionally, you'll want to delete an app, or updates for apps might become available. Here's how to handle these situations.

Rearranging apps in Launcher

To change the order in which apps appear in Launcher, follow these steps:

1. **Tap the Launcher at the bottom of Card View or use the Quick Launch toolbar.**

2. **Tap and hold the icon you want to reposition.**

   A halo appears around the icon; see the Music icon in Figure 15-8.

Halo indicates selected app.

Figure 15-8:
When you
select an
app to
relocate,
it sports a
halo.

3. **After the halo appears, drag the icon to a new position.**

   To move the icon to another page, drag it to the left or right edge of the screen. Don't worry if you misplace it or you need some practice — you can keep running through these steps as many times as you need.

Deleting apps

Occasionally, you'll download an app from the App Catalog that you simply find you don't need or you don't like — or maybe you need to free up some space in your Pre's memory for music or other stuff. Unlike the built-in applications that came with the phone, any apps that you've downloaded can be removed whenever you like.

To delete an app, follow these steps:

1. **Tap the Launcher icon on the Pre main screen.**

2. **Tap the Launcher menu in the upper-left corner of the screen.**

3. **From the menu that appears, choose List Apps (see Figure 15-9).**

The Launcher menu

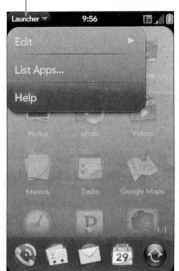

Figure 15-9:
Select List
Apps to see
the apps
you down-
loaded.

4. **In the Preferences list that appears, tap the app you want to delete.**

   Note that downloaded apps appear at the top of the list. Onscreen, two
   choices appear as shown in Figure 15-10. If you just wanted to view information about this application (version number, for example) without
   deleting, you can select Done in this screen.

5. **Tap Delete.**

   Pre asks you to confirm that you want to delete the app.

6. **Tap Delete again.**

   Pre deletes the selected app.

You can use an alternative method to delete an app. From Launcher, swipe
from right to left until you locate the app's icon. (You can get a refresher on
swiping and other gestures in Chapter 3.) Press and hold the Orange key while
you tap the app's icon. The screen shown in Figure 15-10 appears; tap Delete
and then confirm the deletion.

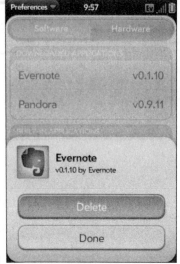

Figure 15-10:
Deleting an
app.

Installing system updates

Occasionally, system updates become available for webOS. No matter what
you're doing at the time, a notification pops up to prompt you to install the
system update. At the bottom of the screen in Figure 15-11, you see a typical
notification that a system update is available.

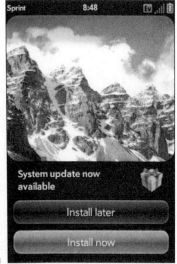

Figure 15-11:
When a
system
update
becomes
available,
a message
appears on
your Pre.

When you tap Install Now, the Pre displays a screen that explains how long you can expect the installation to take; the screen also tells you that you can't use your Pre during that time (see Figure 15-12).

Figure 15-12:
Before you install an update, the Pre indicates how long the update will take.

When you're ready to install the update, tap Install Now, and installation begins. While the update installs, the Pre screen displays the Palm logo and the message `Do not remove the battery`. When the installation finishes, the screen shown in Figure 15-13 appears. Tap Done, and you can go back to using your Pre.

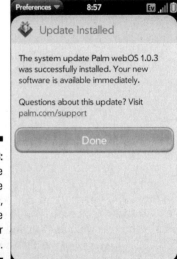

Figure 15-13:
After the update completes, you receive another notification.

Updating apps you downloaded

For apps you download, you might (or might not) receive notifications that updates are available. You can always check the Apps Catalog periodically, though, for updates to the apps you have installed. When you tap an app that you've installed and an update is available, an Update button at the bottom of the screen appears. Tap it and follow the onscreen instructions that appear to install the update.

Updating Your Palm Profile

Your Palm Profile is critical to everything you do on the Pre — so critical, in fact, that until you set it, you can't use your Pre at all! You can transfer an existing Profile from another Palm device to your Pre, so at least you don't have to start from scratch, but until you get your Profile set, you're stuck. Read all about setting your Profile for the first time in Chapter 2.

You can think of a Palm Profile as your phone's alternative to the Palm Desktop — and more. A Palm Profile does the following:

✔ It stores the data in Contacts and your Calendar events and tasks that you create on your Pre.

✔ It stores all your phone's system settings and any applications you download to your phone.

✔ Palm uses it to connect your phone to Palm servers, for example, to get automatic updates and back up your phone's data.

Your Palm Profile doesn't store everything on your Pre. For example, although downloaded apps are a part of your Palm Profile, the data stored in downloaded applications might not be stored in your Palm Profile; check with the app's developer to find out how the app stores information. In addition, information that you transfer from your computer to your Pre using the Pre as a USB drive — stuff like pictures, music, and videos — is not backed up to your Palm Profile. And, finally, your Palm Profile doesn't store any information contained in online calendars, such as Google Microsoft Exchange ActiveSync.

You create a Palm Profile as part of the process of setting up your Palm Pre. If you bought your Pre at a Sprint store, the salesperson probably did that part for you.

You can edit your Palm Profile information at any time either on the Web site or on your phone. The information you can change in your profile includes your first and last name, e-mail address, and security question and answer. You also can change the password you use to gain access to your profile information.

To make changes to your Profile information, follow these steps:

1. **Tap the Launcher icon.**

2. **Swipe from right to left to scroll through the apps until you find the Backup app; tap that.**

3. **Tap Preferences at the very top of the Backup screen.**

4. **On the menu that appears, tap Palm Profile.**

5. **When prompted, enter your Palm Profile password and then tap Done.**

6. **Make your changes.**

   When you're done, simply continue using your Pre — you can navigate away from this screen by going to the Card View, to Launcher, or anywhere else that you like.

You can rename your phone. Tap the Launcher icon. Then swipe from right to left to scroll through the apps until you find the Device Info app; tap that. In the Name field, type a new name.

Safeguarding Your Pre Data

By default, the majority of the information about your Pre is safe because using the webOS Synergy concept, your Pre automatically backs up your Profile every day to the Palm servers.

If you use online calendars (such as Google or Facebook, or Outlook with Microsoft Exchange), the data you store in those calendars remains with those providers, who synchronize your data at regular intervals.

From time to time, bad things happen. That's a fact of life that we can't avoid. On the good news side, though, because your Pre automatically backs itself up daily to the Palm servers, you can easily restore the backed up information should you ever need to erase the data from your phone.

You can turn off Automatic Backup (although I can't think of a good reason to do so), and you can also perform a manual backup — and I *can* think of a good reason to do a manual backup. Suppose, for example, that you want to try out a new app and you're not sure what effect it's going to have on your phone. You can back up your phone before you download and install the app. That way, if the app doesn't play nicely, you can restore your phone to its state before you installed the app.

To manually back up your Pre, follow these steps:

1. **Tap the Launcher icon.**

2. **Swipe from right to left to scroll through the apps until you find the Backup app and tap that.**

3. **At the bottom of the Backup screen that appears (see Figure 15-14), tap Back Up Now.**

   The Pre displays `Preparing` on the button where `Back Up Now` appeared. (*Preparing* actually means "backing up.") When the backup finishes, `Backup Complete` appears on the button.

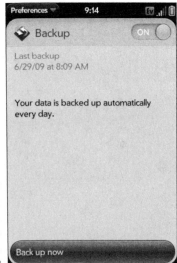

Figure 15-14:
Backing up your Pre manually.

You can see the state of Automatic Backup by looking at the button in the upper-right corner of the Backup screen. If you see `On`, your Pre is automatically backing up daily. You can tap the On button to change the state to Off, but if you do, you'll also erase all backup information stored in your Profile on the Palm server. I recommend that you leave Automatic Backup turned on.

When Things Go Wrong . . .

As mentioned earlier in this chapter, things can go wrong. For example, an application might freeze. When things go wrong, try the following:

1. Restart your phone.

2. Reset your phone.

   This approach also erases all data from your phone.

Restarting your Pre

When you restart your phone, no files or settings are changed. If an app has frozen, try following these steps to restart your phone:

1. **Tap the Launcher icon.**

2. **Swipe from right to left to scroll through the apps until you find the Device Info app; tap that.**

3. **Scroll to the bottom of the information listed and tap Reset Options to display the Reset Options screen shown in Figure 15-15.**

   I'll cover the erase options that you see here later in the chapter.

4. **Tap Restart.**

   The Palm logo appears on your screen. After a few moments, the phone restarts, displaying the main screen.

Figure 15-15: Try restarting your Pre if it freezes.

If the Pre's screen doesn't respond to taps, press and hold the phone's Power button and slide the ringer switch (located at the top of the phone beside the Power button) three times to restart your phone. (For more on powering the Pre on and off, turn to Chapter 2.)

Resetting your Pre

If restarting your phone doesn't solve the problem you're experiencing, reset the phone. Or, if you're planning to give your phone to someone and you don't want that person to have access to your data, you can reset your phone.

Resetting the phone deletes some or all data on your phone, depending on the type of reset you select in the Device Info application (see Figure 15-15):

✓ **Partial Erase:** You can partially erase data from your phone. This option erases all data from the phone except items typically stored in folders on the USB drive, such as pictures, videos, and music.

✓ **Full Erase:** You can erase all data from the phone. This option erases all data for all accounts, including data stored in folders on the USB drive and information about your Palm profile. However, choosing this option doesn't affect any data on the Web in your online accounts and in your Palm profile.

Resetting your phone both erases the data on the phone and restores data stored in your Profile. After you reset your phone, you're prompted to sign in to your Profile; when you do, you automatically initiate a restore of the data stored in your Profile and in your online accounts. However, because your Profile doesn't include data you added to your Pre from your computer, you need to add that data back to your Pre again.

You might want to manually back up your data before resetting your phone. See the section "Safeguarding Your Pre Data," earlier in this chapter, for details on how to manually back up your data.

Here's how to reset your phone:

1. **Tap the Launcher icon.**

2. **Swipe from right to left to scroll through the apps until you find the Device Info app, and tap that.**

3. **Scroll to the bottom of the information listed and tap Reset Options to displays the Reset Options screen shown in Figure 15-15.**

4. **Tap either Partial Erase or Full Erase.**

5. **Tap again the choice you made in Step 4.**

   After resetting your phone, follow the prompts to sign in to your Palm Profile again and begin using your phone. Signing in to your Palm Profile restores your Profile data and information from online accounts, but you'll need to recopy data you loaded from your computer, such as pictures, videos, and music.

Part V
The Part of Tens

The 5th Wave — By Rich Tennant

"Russell! Do you remember last month when I told you to order 150 <u>SMART</u> phones for the sales department?"

In this part . . .

No *For Dummies* title would be able to say goodnight without The Part of Tens — it's a tradition — and you'll find it here. In Chapter 16, you'll see some of my favorite applications for the Pre that are available to download. In Chapter 17, you'll get a look at some great accessories that you can use to make the Pre even cooler than it already is (yes, believe it or not, it's possible!).

And here's the best part: The Pre is so new, so exciting, and so popular that the best applications and accessories are constantly changing — there's always new stuff to explore. So don't just take these lists as your be-all, end-all guide, but use them as a starting point. I promise you won't be disappointed with what you find!

Chapter 16

Ten (Or So) Helpful Applications

· ·

*A*t the time of this writing, the Palm Pre was very new in the marketplace. Seeing as how it sports a brand new operating system from Palm (webOS), it isn't surprising that the market hasn't yet been inundated with apps for the Pre. However, in this chapter, I describe ten apps currently available that I think are worth your notice. All these apps can be found in the App Catalog; see Chapter 15 for details on using the App Catalog.

Bear in mind that at this time, many of the apps available are still works in progress, which means that they'll improve over time — and because the Pre will automatically notify you as new versions of your installed applications become available, staying up to date is a breeze.

Going forward, Palm is doing everything that it can to encourage companies and individual developers to create exciting new applications for the Pre, and by all accounts, it seems that those efforts are working. On your phone, keeping tabs on the latest and greatest software is just a tap away, so keep a close eye on the App Catalog over the coming months to see all of the exciting new apps that become available.

Getting in Sync: PocketMirror for Outlook and The Missing Sync

From Chapura (www.chapura.com), PocketMirror has long been available to Palm OS users. If you're an avid Outlook user, and you want to manage all of your personal information in Outlook, webOS' Synergy feature — which you can read all about in Chapters 8 and 9 — might not be for you, because it can't sync to Outlook on your PC. That's where PocketMirror saves the day because it offers two-way synchronization between your Palm device with the Contacts and Calendar features of Microsoft Outlook. You don't need any cables because PocketMirror synchronizes your PC and your Pre using a local Wi-Fi network. No personal information is stored or passes through the Internet. Chapura is not currently charging for the application while it's in beta.

And from Mark/Space (www.markspace.com), The Missing Sync performs the same synchronization functions between your Pre and your Mac, again, bypassing the Internet. (And a Windows version for PC owners is on the way, too.) It runs $39.95 (or $29.95 if you're upgrading from an older version of The Missing Sync that you purchased for another phone).

Classic

So, you have all these apps you use on your current Palm, but they won't work under the new webOS on your Pre. No need to grumble. Enter Classic from MotionApps, which runs $29.99 (www.motionapps.com/classic/overview). Classic is a Palm OS emulator that enables you to run many of the 30,000 apps already written for the Palm OS on your Pre; see

```
www.motionapps.com/classic/apps/classic_certified_apps
```

Although the Pre doesn't yet have the massive collection of available applications that older Palm OS devices have, you can use Classic to help beef up your app library by continuing to use those older apps. They're still just as good as they used to be!

You can download and install Classic from the Palm App Catalog; it places an application icon into the Launcher just like any other Palm Pre app. Tap the Classic icon, and a Palm OS display appears (see Figure 16-1). To load Palm OS apps (that use PRC files), plug your Pre into your computer; when prompted on the Pre, choose USB disk mode. Then, on your computer, on the drive representing your Pre, you'll find a folder called ClassicApps. Drag and drop the PRC files for apps you want to install into the ClassicApps folder.

As of this writing, Palm OS apps that rely on PDB files (database files, used to store records of information like expense reports, for example) are more complex to install; you need to use a freeware third-party Palm OS app, FileZ (from Nosleep; www.nosleep.net). MotionApps indicates that future versions of Classic will allow you to drag and drop PDB files as well as PRC files.

There's no HotSync support, though, so you can't install any apps that require HotSync. (Think of HotSync as the predecessor to Synergy — it synchronized your device directly with your computer rather than synchronizing it with information on the Internet.) However, Classic comes with a tool to let you enter your HotSync ID for apps that look for a HotSync ID — and as with PDB files, MotionApps says that HotSync will eventually be fully supported. Consult your Palm OS applications' documentation to find out whether they require HotSync.

Figure 16-1:
Classic
displays the
Palm OS on
the Pre so
that you can
run legacy
apps.

Bear in mind that Classic is still a work in progress. MotionApps is working to improve the program's functionality to test and certify new apps everyday. For example, because Classic is an app running on the multitasking Pre, it can slow down your Pre's responses, and you might run into the blue screen of death with some PalmOS apps. If you do, close Classic by throwing its card off the screen (see Chapter 3 for details), and restart it.

SplashID

SplashID from SplashData (www.splashdata.com/splashid/index.asp) is a password manager that helps you track account names and passwords in an organized way. You can store login information, credit card contact information (in case your cards are lost or stolen), membership numbers for rewards programs, bank account numbers — any number you want. And all your treasured identity-related information is encrypted using 256-bit encryption, so it's safe, even if you lose your Pre (heaven forbid!).

This app was still in free beta as of this writing, so I wouldn't recommend that you rely on it just yet. I understand that a desktop version will eventually be available. Using the desktop version, you should be able to import passwords from the Palm OS version of SplashID to avoid retyping all that information, and the desktop version will also enable you to back up your information to your desktop, which is something pretty important when you're talking about identity information.

Tweed

Tweed, an app from Pivotal Labs (http://tweed.pivotallabs.com), is a free Twitter client that enables you to use your Palm Pre to participate in Twitter conversations and explore trends on Twitter. You can reply or re-tweet, search tweets, create bookmarks, and get notifications when you receive messages or replies.

FlightView

Using FlightView (www.flightview.com), available for free in the Apps Catalog, Palm Pre users can plan, monitor, and make informed decisions about travel plans. FlightView uses webOS to give you up-to-the-minute information on the location of a flight (see Figure 16-2). You can track a flight by number or by departure and arrival cities. This app makes it easy to check flight status before departing for the airport and monitor the flight while it's in the air. Arriving passengers can check connection status and gates.

Figure 16-2: Tracking a flight using FlightView.

FlightView also provides status alerts that update you immediately of changes to your flight. In addition, you can add flight details to the Palm Pre calendar.

Express Stocks

Need stock market information? Try Express Stocks from Handmark (www.handmark.com). This free app provides a quick snapshot of major global market indices and financial news; access to market, business, and financial news; and detailed information for each stock ticker, including last trade price, time of last trade, daily change actual and percentage amounts, previous close, opening price for the day, trading range and volume for the day, and trading range for the year. You can set up a personalized stock market portfolio to check prices and company news stories for stocks of interest.

Out and About: GoodFood, WHERE, and Mobile by Citysearch

Location-based apps on the Palm Pre use your location to help you find stuff. Here are three that I really like and find useful. (And the best part: all three are free.)

- ✔ **GoodFood** (from GoodRec; www.goodrec.com) helps you find nearby restaurants. You can sort by price or by cuisine — and, if you want, you can rate restaurants and see what your friends think.

- ✔ **WHERE** (from uLocate Communications; www.where.com) searches for restaurants and much more. WHERE provides local news, weather, gas prices, entertainment, restaurant reviews, and yellow pages listings near your current location using GPS and cell-tower triangulation. And, using built-in Buddy Beacon, you can find out where your friends and family are.

- ✔ **Mobile** by Citysearch (from IAC; www.iac.com) uses your location to find nearby banks, cafes, restaurants, or movie theaters and provides directions via Google Maps. Like with GoodFood and WHERE, you can submit recommendations. You also can share your present location with people in your address book using e-mail, SMS, or Twitter. You can read more about these apps in Chapter 12.

Infopedia

Are you a Wikipedia fan? If so, meet Infopedia, which presents Wikipedia in mobile format on your Palm Pre at no charge. You can use Infopedia to search for anything in Wikipedia from your Palm Pre and receive the information optimized for phone format. Infopedia contains a News button that shows the latest Wikipedia headlines and a Random button that displays a random article if you're just in the mood to learn something new. You can use history and bookmarks to retrieve past searches, and you can e-mail articles to yourself or your friends. The program displays and feels like a Web browser.

AccuWeather

Another location-service app, you can get free AccuWeather information for any location in the world (see Figure 16-3). You can save locations so that you can easily retrieve weather conditions, radar and satellite information, and forecasts. You also can receive alerts for severe weather warnings and get information on how weather will affect activities (like boating and skiing) and conditions like asthma and arthritis. (Be aware that because this app is free, it contains ads.)

Figure 16-3:
Get weather
information.

Fandango

If you're a movie fan, check out Fandango. This app lets you browse movie and theater listings, watch movie trailers, and read fan reviews. Fandango also uses location services to find the theaters closest to you and identifies what's playing at those theaters. And, you can buy tickets using Fandango, add the movie date and time to your calendar, and invite friends to join you at the movie. See Chapter 14 for more on Fandango.

Pandora

Create your own radio station with Pandora. Pandora plays streaming audio from the Internet, but you can use it to set up a radio station that plays the kind of music you like. Read more about using Pandora in Chapter 14.

Chapter 17

Ten (Or So) Palm Pre Accessories

As you might expect, the Palm Pre isn't just a standalone pretty face. It has stuff you can use to dress it up that isn't limited to software. In addition to finding accessories for the Palm Pre at the Palm Web site, the Palm Pre has a Web site devoted to its accessories; visit here to find more accessories as they become available:

```
www.preaccessories.com
```

In this chapter, you'll find descriptions of commonly sought (and helpful) accessories and links to sites where you can find and purchase them. (All prices listed are approximate, in US dollars, and are current as of this writing.)

Palm Pre Spare Battery

If you're one of those "be prepared" types, consider investing in an extra battery for your Palm Pre — one that you can carry with you and swap in at a moment's notice, just in case your phone charge is running low, and you can't stop to charge the phone right now. If you're a very heavy user of the Pre's many features — especially Web browsing, calling, and other functions that use the wireless radio — you might find that you get as little as four hours on a single battery charge. So, for some users, a spare battery is a must.

To purchase an official standard battery manufactured by Palm ($50), visit your network provider's store or the Palm Web site at www.palm.com. A 1350 milliampere-hour (mAh) extended battery for the Palm Pre (as opposed to the standard battery's 1150mAh) is also available from Seidio ($45); visit www.preaccessories.com for details.

Spare Battery Charger

With the spare battery charger, you can charge your Palm Pre's spare battery without installing the battery in the phone. That way, you can have *two* fully charged batteries ready to go: one that you charge while you charge your phone, and one that you charge separately from your phone.

To purchase a spare battery charger ($30), visit your local Sprint store, the Palm Web site at www.palm.com, or the Palm Pre accessories site at www.preaccessories.com.

Palm Pre Chargers

Palm's Touchstone charging systems enable you to charge your Palm Pre without connecting any wires directly to your phone. How cool is that? Instead, you use the Palm International Power Charger that comes with the Palm Pre to connect the charging base to a power source. Remove the battery cover that came on your Pre and attach the Touchstone Back Cover. Inductive coils inside the charging dock generate and transmit a small, oscillating electromagnetic field through the back cover so that you can charge the Palm Pre without connecting any wires to it directly. Sweet.

When you set your Palm Pre into the charging dock, it snaps into place magnetically and begins charging. While in the charging dock, nightstand mode automatically displays the time and incoming notifications.

You can also talk on the Pre while the phone is charging in the dock. The phone's speakerphone automatically turns on while it's in the charging dock; if you remove the phone from the dock, the call automatically transfers back to the phone's earpiece.

Touchstone Technology also answers incoming calls automatically (you don't need to tap the screen) when you lift the phone from the charging dock.

When you buy a Pre, it doesn't come with a Touchstone — you need to charge it the old-fashioned way. Where's the fun in that? The good news is that you can purchase three different versions of Touchstone Charging kits.

- **Touchstone Charging Kit ($70):** Includes the Palm Touchstone Charging Dock and the Palm Touchstone Back Cover.

- **Touchstone Charging Expansion Kit ($80):** Includes one Touchstone Charging Dock and one Palm International Power Charger. Using the expansion kit, you can charge your phone in two physical locations — say home and office — without needing to carry charging equipment with you.

- **Touchstone Dual Location Charging Kit ($140):** A combo of the first two kits. It includes two charging docks, one International Power Charger (remember that one comes automatically with the phone), and one Touchstone Back Cover. That's all the hardware you need to charge your Palm Pre in two separate physical locations.

You don't need to purchase a dock/charger bundle. You can purchase the Touchstone Charging Dock, the International Power Charger cable, and the Touchstone Back Cover separately. At the time of this writing, though, you tend to do better price-wise if you buy a kit.

To purchase Touchstone charging accessories, visit your network provider's store, the Palm Web site at `www.palm.com`, or the Palm Pre accessories site at `www.preaccessories.com`.

Travel Chargers

Palm makes a travel charger for the Palm Pre that can be used in the United States, the United Kingdom, Europe, Australia, and Argentina. Seidio also makes a high-output folding travel charger that works only in the United States.

To purchase a travel charger, visit your local network provider's store or the Palm Web site.

Vehicle Chargers

And don't forget the ever-handy car charger: the one you use to charge your phone while you drive. The Palm Vehicle Power Charger includes a removable 2½ foot micro-USB cable. Similar car chargers are available from Smartphone Experts, Motorola, and Seidio at `http://store.precentral.net`, `www.store.motorola.com`, and `www.seidio.com`, respectively.

To purchase a vehicle charger, visit your local network provider's store, the Palm Web site, or the Palm Pre accessories site.

International Power Charger

The International Power Charger ($40) is a compact charging system for your Pre that can be used in a variety of countries around the world. This charger automatically adjusts voltage and frequency, and you get adaptor plugs that handle voltage ranging between 100 and 240 volts (V), covering different currents in the United States, the United Kingdom, Australia, Argentina, and Europe.

You can purchase the Palm International Power Charger from Sprint or the Palm Web site. Seidio also makes a high-output folding travel charger for Palm Pre; read about it at the Palm Pre accessories site at `www.pre accessories.com`.

Micro-USB Cable

Use the 5-foot micro-USB cable from Palm to connect your Pre to the Palm Vehicle Power Charger to the AC Power Adapter, or directly to a computer (which is a super-convenient way to get a quick charge when you don't have a charger handy).

Seidio also makes a charging USB cable, and Smartphone Experts makes a retractable cable that both syncs and charges the Palm Pre.

Cases for the Palm Pre

Smartphone Experts offer an all-leather, top-pouch carrying case ($25) and an all-leather, side-pouch carrying case (also $25) for the Palm Pre; both cases come in a variety of colors and sport a leather belt clip and a magnetic closure.

In addition to cases, Smartphone Experts sells screen protectors ($15) for the Pre. All these products can be found at `http://store.precentral.net`.

A holster-style case from Seidio ($30) is available for the Pre; this rubberized coated holster is made of polycarbonate, making it durable. The Palm Pre fits face-in to the holder to help protect the screen. The holster also provides easy access to connectors. Seidio also makes a case without a clip called the Innocase Surface ($30) if you don't need to clip the Pre to your belt. The great thing about this particular case is that it's fully compatible with the Touchstone. Unlike most cases, you can dock your Pre to the Touchstone without removing it from the Innocase. These cases can be found at the Seidio Web site (`www.seidio.com`).

The Body Glove is a universal protective case that has a horizontal fit and a low profile clip that attaches to your belt, pocket, or purse.

Two leather cases are available from Palm:

- **Slip case:** A black Nappa leather pouch with a splash of color inside; this case has no belt clip. The Slip Case retains its shape when you pull out your phone.

- **Slide case:** Also made of black Nappa leather; includes a belt clip, a magnetic closure, and a leather-reinforced ribbon you can use to pull your phone out of the case. The inside of this case is soft microfiber.

Palm Pre Stereo Headset

Use the Palm Pre Stereo 3.5mm headset with ear buds to listen to music or talk on the phone. If you happen to be listening to music when a call comes in, you can switch to phone mode using the Answer/End call button on the headset's control box. The ear buds contain magnets that you can use to clasp the buds together at the back of your neck when you aren't using them.

The Pre includes a pair of these in the box, but let's be honest. Headsets are easy to lose, and it's always a good idea to have a second pair lying around. You can keep one at home and pack another in your briefcase, purse, or backpack, for example. To purchase the Palm Pre Stereo headset ($25), visit your local network provider's store or the Palm Web site.

Bluetooth Headsets

With the Plantronics Voyager 855 ($85) stereo Bluetooth headset — a mere 15 grams — you can listen to music and switch to calls when necessary. This headset features a sliding boom to get your voice closer to the microphone so that you can be heard more clearly; you also can use the sliding boom to answer and end calls. You typically can get approximately 7 hours of talk time and 160 hours of standby time from a single charge.

The Jawbone PRIME Bluetooth headset ($130) works with the Pre as well as some of the older Palm phones; it features special technology and circuitry that helps to reduce background noise by detecting vibrations in your face that correspond to your voice (sounds like science fiction, doesn't it?)

The Sennheiser FLX70 Bluetooth headset uses an "in-ear" design that sports no ear hook. In the package, you'll find an optional ear hook; lanyard you can use to keep the headset handy without keeping it in your ear; a wall charger and USB charge cable; and small, medium, and large ear buds.

The MOTOROKR S305 Wireless Stereo Headphones use Bluetooth technology and enables you to listen to music and take or make a call. You can control your music from the headphone using track and volume controls.

The BlueAnt S1 is a Bluetooth headset that can be voice activated; for example, to answer a call, you can respond, "Answer," "Accept Call," or "Okay."

To purchase a Bluetooth headset for your Palm Pre, visit your local Sprint store, the Palm Web site at www.palm.com, or the Palm Pre accessories site at www.preaccessories.com.

Bluetooth Hands-free Speakerphone

The speakerphone that's built into the Pre is alright for occasional use, but if you find yourself frequently holding conference calls with several others in the room with you or you're taking calls from your car and you don't want to have a Bluetooth headset stuck in your ear all the time, a Bluetooth hands-free speakerphone might be just what the doctor ordered.

Palm (http://store.palm.com) sells an excellent Bluetooth speakerphone — the Supertooth 3, from BlueAnt — that can clip right to your car's sun visor so that's always easily accessible while you're driving. Using this speakerphone is safer (and can keep you legal in those states with laws regarding using a phone in the car) than talking with the phone held to your face. It's available for $100.

Index

• B •

Business/Accounting & Bookkeeping

Bookkeeping For Dummies
978-0-7645-9848-7

eBay Business
All-in-One For Dummies,
2nd Edition
978-0-470-38536-4

Job Interviews
For Dummies,
3rd Edition
978-0-470-17748-8

Resumes For Dummies,
5th Edition
978-0-470-08037-5

Stock Investing
For Dummies,
3rd Edition
978-0-470-40114-9

Successful Time
Management
For Dummies
978-0-470-29034-7

Computer Hardware

BlackBerry For Dummies,
3rd Edition
978-0-470-45762-7

Computers For Seniors
For Dummies
978-0-470-24055-7

iPhone For Dummies,
2nd Edition
978-0-470-42342-4

Laptops For Dummies,
3rd Edition
978-0-470-27759-1

Macs For Dummies,
10th Edition
978-0-470-27817-8

Cooking & Entertaining

Cooking Basics
For Dummies,
3rd Edition
978-0-7645-7206-7

Wine For Dummies,
4th Edition
978-0-470-04579-4

Diet & Nutrition

Dieting For Dummies,
2nd Edition
978-0-7645-4149-0

Nutrition For Dummies,
4th Edition
978-0-471-79868-2

Weight Training
For Dummies,
3rd Edition
978-0-471-76845-6

Digital Photography

Digital Photography
For Dummies,
6th Edition
978-0-470-25074-7

Photoshop Elements 7
For Dummies
978-0-470-39700-8

Gardening

Gardening Basics
For Dummies
978-0-470-03749-2

Organic Gardening
For Dummies,
2nd Edition
978-0-470-43067-5

Green/Sustainable

Green Building
& Remodeling
For Dummies
978-0-4710-17559-0

Green Cleaning
For Dummies
978-0-470-39106-8

Green IT For Dummies
978-0-470-38688-0

Health

Diabetes For Dummies,
3rd Edition
978-0-470-27086-8

Food Allergies
For Dummies
978-0-470-09584-3

Living Gluten-Free
For Dummies
978-0-471-77383-2

Hobbies/General

Chess For Dummies,
2nd Edition
978-0-7645-8404-6

Drawing For Dummies
978-0-7645-5476-6

Knitting For Dummies,
2nd Edition
978-0-470-28747-7

Organizing For Dummies
978-0-7645-5300-4

SuDoku For Dummies
978-0-470-01892-7

Home Improvement

Energy Efficient Homes
For Dummies
978-0-470-37602-7

Home Theater
For Dummies,
3rd Edition
978-0-470-41189-6

Living the Country Lifestyle
All-in-One For Dummies
978-0-470-43061-3

Solar Power Your Home
For Dummies
978-0-470-17569-9

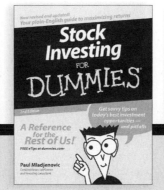

Available wherever books are sold. For more information or to order direct: U.S. customers visit www.dummies.com or call 1-877-762-2974.
U.K. customers visit www.wileyeurope.com or call (0) 1243 843291. Canadian customers visit www.wiley.ca or call 1-800-567-4797.

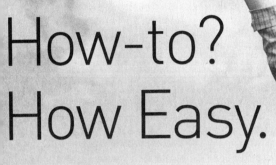

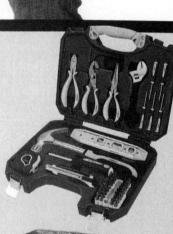

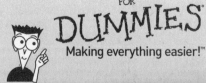